For the Love of Salad

For the Love of Salad

• JEANELLE MITCHELL •

whitecap

Whitecap Books is known for its expertise in the cookbook market, and has produced some of the most
innovative and familiar titles found in kitchens across North America. Visit our website at www.whitecap.ca.

Edited by Paula Ayer
Cover design by Michelle Furbacher
Interior design by Grace Partridge
Illustrations by Jeanelle Mitchell

Printed in Canada at Friesens

Library and Archives Canada Cataloguing in Publication

Mitchell, Jeanelle
      For the love of salad / Jeanelle Mitchell.

ISBN 978-1-77050-007-5

      1. Salads. I. Title.

TX740.M58 2010   641.8'3   C2009-906415-4

The publisher acknowledges the financial support of the Government of Canada through the Canada
Book Fund (CBF) and the Province of British Columbia through the Book Publishing Tax Credit.

11 12 13 14   5 4 3 2

Contents

This book is dedicated to my nephew, Yves, who is severely handicapped due to an auto accident. Proceeds of this book will go to assist Yves with therapy and other needs. With love to my sister and her family.

Preface

My passion for fine food began during my globe-trotting days as a flight attendant, and today I continue to enjoy foods from many cultures. My first cookbook, *For the Love of Soup* (2002), was inspired by my passion for nutritious, satisfying comfort food and continues to get rave reviews from readers. Now, my obsession with fresh, seasonal food has inspired me to write *For the Love of Salad*. Writing this cookbook has brought me a great deal of pleasure; I am always excited to try new food, experiment with different flavours, and, best of all, create new dishes. It is wonderful that ingredients from around the world can now be found at most supermarkets and greengrocers.

This cookbook is all about salads—Mother Nature's "superfood." Salads are brimming with essential vitamins and minerals and fit perfectly with today's emphasis on lighter and healthier eating. Canada's Food Guide recommends at least seven daily servings of fruits and vegetables for adults. The reason: they provide your body with a wide variety of proven disease-fighting substances—and they taste great! Salad ingredients are rich in antioxidants, which protect cells against damage caused by free radicals and are associated with a lower risk of cancer. Salads are also ideal for those who want to limit their calorie and fat consumption.

The recipes here take a fresh approach to eating "good for you" foods that are satisfying and bursting with flavour. Plan your meals around what is in season and buy locally grown food whenever possible to guarantee nourishing and flavourful salads. The secret to extraordinary salads lies in their ingredients, and good quality is the key.

Salads can also help to teach your children healthy eating habits. By introducing children to a broad variety of interesting and tasty salad foods, you can leave them with a legacy of healthy living!

I believe that the taste, smell, and visual beauty of food not only give us pleasure but enrich the soul as well. And food is enjoyed most when it's shared. May these easy-to-prepare recipes inspire you to create fresh and delicious salads throughout the year and enjoy memorable dining experiences with your family and friends.

Eat, love, and laugh. Cheers to good health and happiness with every bite!

Tips
for Successful Salads

In this chapter, you'll find everything you need to get started with making delicious, unique salads— from how to choose and prepare your greens, vegetables, and herbs to the kitchen equipment that will make preparing salads a breeze. You'll also find out how to make fantastic dressings from scratch by starting with a few basic recipes and personalizing with your favourite oils, vinegars, and flavouring ingredients.

Buying and Preparing Leafy Greens

Ranging in flavour from mild to bitter and in texture from buttery to crisp, the greens you select will have a big impact on your final salad. Mix and match different lettuce varieties for eye-catching salads that deliver fresh taste.

To *select salad greens*, look for leaves that are fresh, bright, and crisp. Choose lettuce heads that are densely packed and heavy for their size. As with other plant foods, the fresher the greens, the higher their concentration of nutrients and antioxidants—not to mention the best flavour. Buy greens and herbs from your local farmers' market if you can—you'll be guaranteed freshness.

To *prepare greens*, trim stem ends and discard any exterior leaves that show signs of wear and tear. To wash, separate the leaves, immerse them in a large bowl or sink filled with cool water, and give them a generous swish. Lift out the leaves and shake them gently. Place them in a salad spinner and dry well (vinaigrettes adhere best to dry greens).

To *store greens*, after washing and drying, wrap the leaves in paper towels and store them in a plastic bag in the refrigerator until ready to use. Salad greens can be stored for five to six days, depending on their initial freshness. Greens with soft-textured leaves, such as Boston lettuce, bibb lettuce, and young arugula, spoil within a few days. Other varieties, such as romaine, iceberg, and red leaf lettuce, hold up better. Leaf lettuces are now available from hydroponic greenhouses with the roots attached, which lengthens their refrigerator life. They cost a little more but are well worth it. Greens with sharper and more pungent flavours, such as watercress, radicchio, Belgian endive, and young spinach, keep well. (Remove any large stems from watercress, leaving the smaller stems attached.)

Organic option

Whenever you can, purchase organic and minimize your exposure to pesticides. Organic fruits and vegetables can contain up to 50 percent more antioxidants than conventionally grown fruits and vegetables.

Mild greens

Boston and bibb lettuces have a buttery-smooth texture with sweet, mild leaves and a fresh taste. Romaine lettuce has crisp leaves with a strong, fresh taste and a pleasing crunch. Pale iceberg lettuce has a high percentage of water and is rather bland (I mostly use iceberg lettuce in sandwiches to add a crunch). The delicate leaves of mâche (also called lamb's lettuce) have a mild, subtly sweet, and nutty taste. Mâche is a lovely fall and winter green that comes in small bunches. Loose leaf lettuces (oak leaf, green leaf, and red leaf) have distinctively notched leaves and are light in flavour. Spinach has tender leaves with a rich, earthy flavour. Baby spinach has a milder flavour and a more delicate texture than regular spinach. If you are buying spinach in bunches, wash it thoroughly to remove all the grit.

Bitter and peppery greens

Belgian endive has a light, bittersweet, but delicate flavour and is crunchy and juicy. Frisée (also called curly endive) and escarole are bittersweet and sharper. Radicchio is mildly bitter with a spicy undertone. Arugula, also known as rocket, is an Italian green that's distinguished by its tangy, peppery bite. Its intensity depends on the maturity of the plant. Baby arugula is best, but if you can't find it, buy the larger arugula leaves, remove the stems, and chop the leaves coarsely. Watercress is an aquatic plant that has small, dark green leaves and a spicy, peppery bite.

Packaged salad greens

You can buy packaged, pre-washed mixed salad greens in the produce section of many supermarkets, in varieties including mesclun, European, baby greens, or field greens. Mesclun is the French name for a mixture of salad leaves that usually includes arugula, mâche, oak leaf, frisée, radicchio, and baby romaine leaves. Often, a few herbs, such as chervil and Italian parsley, are also included. You can make your own mesclun by combining your favourite types of lettuce with other salad greens. Asian salad mix usually combines tatsoi, mizuna, baby spinach, and other greens and is excellent in all kinds of salads, even if they are not Asian inspired. You can find the most interesting, flavourful mixes at farmers' markets.

Buying and Preparing Fresh Vegetables

While many fruits and vegetables are available year round, most are at their peak during specific seasons. This guide will help you create your recipes around what is in season.

Buying seasonal produce

SPRING	SUMMER	AUTUMN	WINTER
apricots	beets	apples	avocados
arugula	broccoli	beets	cabbage
asparagus	blackberries	Belgian endive	celery
avocados	blueberries	broccoli	clementines
carrots	carrots	butternut squash	fennel
chives	corn	carrots	grapefruit
fennel	cucumber	cauliflower	leeks
fiddleheads	eggplant	celeriac	lemons
mango	green and	figs	mandarins
new potatoes	yellow beans	garlic	onions
pineapple	nectarines	ginger	oranges
radishes	peaches	grapes	pomegranates
spinach	peppers	mushrooms	potatoes
spring baby	raspberries	parsnips	radicchio
lettuce	spinach	pears	radishes
strawberries	summer squash	pomegranates	tangerines
sugar snap peas	tomatoes	sweet potatoes	
snow peas	watermelon		
Vidalia onions			
watercress			

Tips for buying, storing, and preparing fresh produce

Always buy fresh produce that looks its best, and avoid blemished, bruised, or dried-out fruits and vegetables. Buy local, seasonal produce whenever possible. I like using a fruit and vegetable wash, sold in a spray bottle. It is wonderful for cleaning away dirt, wax, water-repellent agricultural chemicals, and fingerprints from your fruits and vegetables.

- Store mushrooms in paper bags, as plastic makes them sweat, turning them slimy. Poke a couple of holes in the paper bag so that the air can pass through, and the mushrooms should keep three to four days. Do not clean until just before use. Avoid submerging mushrooms in water; wash them under cool running water and immediately dry them with paper towels, or wipe them individually with a wet paper towel.

- Store potatoes, squash, onions, and garlic loose, in a cool, dark place.

- To ripen avocados, mangoes, pears, or tomatoes, place them in a fruit bowl on the kitchen counter for two to four days. To speed up the ripening process, you can place them in a paper bag at room temperature. A ripe fruit yields to gentle pressure. Once ripened, keep avocados, mangoes, and pears in the refrigerator. The fruit is best sliced or diced at the last minute to prevent it from browning. Tomatoes should not be stored in the refrigerator, as this will decrease their flavour and alter their texture.

- To peel a mango, before cutting, wash the mango with the peel on. Use a sharp knife to carefully cut the fruit in half vertically, sliding the knife along the seed. Repeat this on the other side so you have two halves. Slice the halves while still in the peel, then turn the mango halves inside out to fan out the fruit. Slice off the fruit at the base.

- To open an avocado, cut it in half lengthwise, through to the pit. Separate the halves by twisting them in opposite directions. Remove the pit by hitting it with the blade of your knife and twisting. After removing the pit, scoop the flesh out from each side in one piece with a large spoon.

- To section oranges and grapefruit, with a sharp knife, remove the peel and pith from the fruit, first by cutting off the top and bottom, then by slicing off the sides along the contours. Trim off any remaining pith, which is bitter. Cut between the fruit segments and membranes to remove each section.

Buying locally raised food

Buying locally raised food is a crucial trend. Less travel time means less impact on the environment. By supporting local farmers today, you can help ensure that there will be farms in your community tomorrow and that future generations will have access to nourishing, flavourful, and abundant food. Everywhere there are farmers, there are farmers' markets not far away, which, not surprisingly, are the best places to buy locally grown produce. Most farmers' markets also sell locally raised meat and eggs. Some indoor markets carry on through the winter.

- To open a pomegranate, slice off the crown. Lightly score the fruit into quarters, from crown to stem end. Fill a large bowl with water. Submerge the fruit and, keeping it underwater, break it apart, gently separating the seeds from the outer skin and white pith. The seeds will drop to the bottom of the bowl, and the pith will float to the surface. Discard the pith. Pour the seeds into a colander, rinse, and pat dry.

- To roast sweet red (or yellow) peppers, preheat a broiler or barbecue grill. Roast the peppers whole under the broiler or on the grill until the skins are charred black. Place in a bowl and cover with plastic wrap for 15 minutes. Peel the peppers and remove the stems and seeds. You can keep roasted peppers covered with a little olive oil in the refrigerator for at least a week to serve with other salads, in sandwiches, or in soup.

- To roast beets, scrub and trim beets, leaving 1 inch (2.5 cm) of stems attached. Position a rack in the centre of the oven and preheat to 400°F (200°C). Wrap the beets individually in foil. Roast them until tender when pierced with a knife, about 1 hour and 15 minutes. When the beets are cool enough to handle, trim the tops and bottoms. Peel under cold running water; the peel will slip off easily. Chill the beets before adding them to your salad. The beets can be roasted and peeled a day or two before serving and stored in a sealed container in the refrigerator. (Alternatively, cook the beets in a large saucepan of boiling water until tender, about 50 minutes.)

Using Fresh Herbs

Fresh herbs will enhance any salad, providing it with distinctive flavour. Herbs offer more than taste; they are rich in antioxidants and other healing compounds. Many herbs also have a substantial amount of vitamins A and K.

Choosing and preparing herbs

To keep your herbs fresh, treat them like a bouquet of flowers. Immerse the stems in a jar with 2 inches (5 cm) of water. Cover loosely with a plastic bag and refrigerate. Change the water occasionally—the herbs will stay fresh for several days. Before using, rinse the herbs under cold running water and dry thoroughly by gently patting with paper towels. If the leaves are attached to woody stems, pull them off the stems and then chop.

The taste of parsley is described as clean and refreshing. The flat-leaf, or Italian, variety is more strongly flavoured than the curly variety. Parsley has a celery-like taste and is very popular because it underlines the aroma of foods without being dominant. High in vitamins A and C, parsley is also known as a natural breath freshener. Basil is peppery in taste and has a faint tang of cloves and anise. Cilantro (fresh coriander) has a pungent, palate-awakening taste, with hints of citrus. Mint is sweet and has a cool, refreshing taste. Chives (first up in my spring garden) have a light onion-like taste. Their edible purple flowers make a pretty garnish for your salads. Thyme is an herb with tiny leaves and a minty, tea-like flavour. Rosemary has a pungent but sweet taste and a piney scent. Tarragon has a mild licorice taste. Chervil is a sweet, aromatic herb that also has a mild taste of licorice. Dill has a delicate, mild caraway flavour. Greek oregano has a spicy, piquant taste.

Edible flowers are a beautiful garnish for salads. I have found nasturtiums among the most versatile. I make sure to plant my own nasturtiums annually—that way I know they're safe to eat. Nasturtium petals will add a light mustard taste to your salad.

Salad Extras

Adding extras like eggs, meats, and nuts to your salad provides protein and different textures, and can help turn your salad into a satisfying meal. Here are some ideas for salad additions to get you started.

Hard-boiled eggs

Place eggs in a single layer in a medium saucepan. Add enough cold water to cover the eggs by 1 inch (2.5 cm). Place on medium-high heat until the water comes to a rapid boil. Remove from the heat, cover, and let stand for 15 minutes. Drain the eggs and run cold water over them in the pan until they are cooled.

Another method is to bring a saucepan of water to a boil, using enough water to cover the eggs by 1 inch (2.5 cm). With a slotted spoon, slowly lower the eggs into the water. Reduce the heat to a simmer and cook the eggs for 12 minutes. Drain the eggs and run cold water over them in the pan until they are cooled.

Nuts and seeds

Nuts are emerging as nutritional superstars as scientists continue to discover their positive health benefits. Most nuts are rich in vitamin E and potassium and are a good source of other minerals and fibre.

Toasting intensifies the flavour of nuts and seeds and makes every dish they are added to taste that much better. Health food stores tend to have the best retail turnover for nuts. Store shelled nuts in the freezer in an airtight bag—freezing prevents nut oils from turning rancid. To keep the crunch, hold off on adding nuts to your salad until just before serving.

To toast nuts, place the rack in the centre of the oven and preheat the oven to 350°F (180°C). Place the nuts on a rimmed baking sheet and toast for 6 to 8 minutes, or until lightly browned and fragrant. An alternate method is to place the nuts in a small skillet and toast over medium heat, stirring constantly, for 5 to 7 minutes, until golden and fragrant. To toast small nuts (such as pine nuts), slivered almonds, or seeds, place them in a dry skillet over medium heat, shaking the pan constantly for 3 to 4 minutes, or until they are golden and fragrant. Toasted nuts can be stored in an airtight container or Ziploc bag for several days.

Croutons

Croutons add an interesting contrast in texture as well as flavour to your salad. Use day-old bread for easy slicing, and remember that any kind of bread can be used. Sourdough, pumpernickel, rye, whole wheat, or crusty bread are all great choices.

Cut the crusts off the bread, brush with olive oil or melted butter, and cut into small cubes (or make shapes using cookie cutters to turn your salad presentation into a work of art).

Spread bread cubes on a baking sheet and place in a 350°F (180°C) oven. Bake, tossing croutons occasionally, for about 8 to 10 minutes, or until golden brown and crisp. (To make herbed croutons, sprinkle a small amount of your favourite dried herb on the bread cubes before baking.) Croutons will keep in an airtight container at room temperature for about 4 days. If the stored croutons lose crispness, bake them at 300°F (150°C) for 3 to 5 minutes before serving.

Pita crisps

Pita bread is especially tasty when cut into wedges and lightly toasted. It makes an excellent accompaniment for salads.

Preheat the oven to 400°F (200°C). Split pita breads in half horizontally, brush lightly with olive oil, and cut into wedges. Spread pita wedges in a single layer on a large baking sheet. Bake pita wedges, flipping after 5 minutes, then bake again until crisp and slightly browned, another 5 to 6 minutes. (To make garlic pita crisps, combine 1 minced garlic clove with 2 Tbsp (30 mL) olive oil and brush on pitas before cutting into wedges and baking.) Let cool before serving. They will keep in an airtight container at room temperature for about 4 days. If the stored pitas lose crispness, bake at 300°F (150°C) for 3 to 5 minutes before serving.

Meat and seafood

Buy meat and fish from reliable butchers or markets, and buy fish on the day you intend to cook it. Make sure that the fish has a firm appearance and a delicate aroma of the sea.

Barbecuing tips

Always oil either the grill or the food before placing the food on the grill. This prevents the food from sticking.

Keep an eye on the meat, poultry, or seafood while cooking in case the fat catches fire and there are flare-ups. Keep a spray bottle of water beside you to put out the flames.

Grill with the lid down to speed up cooking. Once the lid is closed, the barbecue acts like an oven as well as a grill, cooking foods more quickly. Marinate food outside the refrigerator for up to an hour. Longer marinating should be done in the refrigerator.

Other salad additions

CAPERS are small flower buds that grow on a bush native to the Mediterranean. They have a sharp, tangy flavour that is a pleasant addition to some salads. You will find capers in the condiment section of your supermarket.

SUN-DRIED TOMATOES have a slightly chewy texture. They add a concentrated tomato taste and slight sweetness to salads.

ANCHOVIES should be packed in good olive oil. Once you've opened a tin or jar of anchovies, store the remainder covered in olive oil in the refrigerator, where they will keep perfectly for several months. If you buy anchovies in salt, rinse them well before using in salads or dressings. Salty and yummy! Plus, anchovies are full of omega-3 fatty acids.

OLIVES are found in many different varieties at most deli counters, packed in brine or oil. The canned variety usually does not have much flavour. Dry-cured olives are black, wrinkled, and tasty, with a meaty texture. Greek kalamata olives are purple-black and shiny, with an elegant almond shape. They are considered superior olives. They are brine cured, plump, juicy, and salty. Niçoise olives are tiny, tart, red-brown olives from France. They are brine cured and packed in olive oil, with a nutty, mellow taste. Niçoise olives have a higher pit-to-meat ratio and should be left whole, if using. To pit other varieties, apply pressure with the side of your knife, then slit once to slip out the pit.

PARMESAN CHEESE is rich and complex in flavour, with a pleasant granular texture. For freshness, buy a wedge of Parmesan that has just been sliced from a wheel. For shavings, draw a vegetable peeler or small knife across a block of cheese to create thin sheets and curls. A sprinkling of good-quality Parmesan cheese goes a long way to give a great salad a final touch with its slightly sharp, nutty flavour.

Dressing for Success

The flavour of the dressing is critical to the success of any salad. Dressings complement the texture and aroma of the salad, accent its sharpness, and bring out delicate flavours. A good salad dressing should enhance and harmonize with the simple, fresh tastes of a salad. Dressings can be as creative and varied as salads themselves. Once you realize just how quick, easy, and adaptable salad dressing is, you will rarely pick a bottle off a grocery shelf.

Allow the dressing's flavours to develop by making your dressing earlier in the day, then covering and refrigerating it. (Most dressings can be made up to four days ahead.) There's nothing like having a few salad dressings on hand when you're entertaining or feeding your family.

Most dressings are a combination of an oil, an acid (vinegar or citrus), and flavouring ingredients. The basic balance is three parts oil to one part acid, but this may vary depending on the flavour and strength of both the oil and vinegar used. Oil and vinegar do not hold together; therefore, the process of combining dressing ingredients involves making an emulsion. Mustard, for example, is used in many types of vinaigrette not only for its flavour but also for its emulsifying properties. Eggs are used as an emulsifier when mixing oil with vinegar or lemon juice to make mayonnaise. (Store-bought mayonnaise is generally preferred these days, to avoid any risk associated with the raw eggs used in homemade mayonnaise.)

Salad dressings fall into two general categories: vinaigrettes (oil and acid, whether vinegar or citrus) and creamy dressings (based on mayonnaise, yogurt, sour cream, or buttermilk). The basic recipes on pages 18 and 19 can be varied by experimenting with different oils, acids, and flavourings.

Oils & vinegars

A selection of good-quality oils and vinegars is truly essential for creating delicious salads. Here is a list of my favourite oils and vinegars.

Oils

Buy your oil in small bottles and store away from heat and light. Discard any oil that's been in your cupboard for six months or longer, unless it hasn't been opened.

EXTRA VIRGIN OLIVE OIL is considered the finest and fruitiest of the olive oils. In order to qualify as extra virgin olive oil, the olives must undergo only cold pressing, possess an acidity level of less than 1 percent, and have a perfectly balanced taste. Bright green oils are peppery and a little bitter, while yellow oils are warmer and have a buttery flavour. Take a taste test to find one that suits you.

GRAPESEED OIL is a good alternative to olive oil when you're seeking a light and delicate flavour. This lightweight, pale oil is gaining popularity for its versatility in cooking and its health benefits. It is cholesterol free and contains no sodium. Like olive oil, it has been shown to raise levels of HDL (good) cholesterol and reduce levels of LDL (bad) cholesterol.

SAFFLOWER OIL is also a healthy choice, but it would be my second choice, as grapeseed oil is more flavourful and versatile.

WALNUT OIL is deep flavoured, with rich aromas. It is best mixed with grapeseed or olive oil. Because it is affected by light and exposure to air, walnut oil should be kept refrigerated after opening.

SESAME OIL is a key ingredient in Asian cooking. It is a strong-tasting oil made from toasted sesame seeds and has a nut-like flavour. Use it sparingly in dressings—a little goes a long way. Store in the refrigerator once opened.

Vinegars

The name *vinegar* comes from the French words *vin aigre*, meaning "sour wine."

SHERRY VINEGAR is wonderful in any salad. This Spanish vinegar is made from sherry wine. It is full bodied and less acidic than other wine vinegars.

BALSAMIC VINEGAR is dark in colour, very smooth, and mellow, with deep complexity and subtle flavours. The production of balsamic vinegar dates back to the Middle Ages. It is produced by fermenting and aging white grape juice in wood casks similar to those used in winemaking.

APPLE CIDER VINEGAR is made from fermented apples and is rich in nutrients such as potassium. It is a tart, fruity vinegar that lets the taste of salad greens shine through.

RED WINE VINEGAR has a sharp, sweet, full-bodied flavour and, if wood aged, a slightly smoky undertone. It complements tangy greens.

WHITE WINE VINEGAR has a sweeter, cleaner taste than red wine vinegar and combines well with milder-tasting greens. Often, I prefer using cider vinegar to using white wine vinegar.

CHAMPAGNE VINEGAR is fermented from sparkling white wine. It has a slightly sweet flavour with a hint of tartness. Champagne vinegar can be hard to find and is also expensive. If you can't find it, I would suggest using good-quality white wine vinegar or cider vinegar instead.

RICE WINE VINEGAR is made from fermented rice. It is most commonly associated with Asian cooking. Rice wine vinegar has a mild, fruity flavour. I like using the unseasoned variety for salads. You can substitute with apple cider vinegar.

Flavouring ingredients for dressings

The beautiful thing about homemade dressings is the ability to get creative. Vary the taste of a basic vinaigrette or basic creamy dressing by adding flavouring ingredients to enliven, brighten, sweeten, or give an extra punch.

FRESH HERBS such as parsley, basil, oregano, tarragon, mint, thyme, cilantro, or dill will heighten any salad dressing with their distinctive flavours. Experiment with different combinations of herbs.

CITRUS (lemon, lime, or orange) is a good way to put some zing into your salad dressings. It is a great flavour enhancer and can bring out the best aroma from other ingredients without overpowering them. Add the zest of fresh lemon, lime, or orange to your dressings for extra tang.

SHALLOTS are small purple onions that are more delicate in taste than cooking onions and add a great kick to salads and dressings.

GARLIC is a natural seasoning and will enhance the flavour of your dressing. Not only will garlic spice up your salads and wake up your taste buds, it will also improve your health; garlic is a powerful antioxidant. If you like the taste of garlic but find it too strong, try rubbing the inside of your salad bowl with a clove of garlic.

HONEY dissolves easily and makes an excellent addition to homemade dressings, acting as a sweet agent to contrast with more savoury flavours. In addition to being irresistibly sweet, honey inhibits bacteria growth and contains disease-fighting antioxidants. To revive crystallized honey, open a glass honey jar, place it in a saucepan filled with 1 inch (2.5 cm) of water, and heat until the crystals are dissolved.

MAPLE SYRUP is an ingredient I love to use in salad dressings because it is natural and adds an earthy sweetness to vinaigrettes. On average, it takes 40 gallons of maple sap to produce one gallon of syrup. Maple syrup provides traces of vitamins, potassium, and calcium.

DIJON MUSTARD adds a sharp flavour to dressings and also acts as a binder to help emulsify vinaigrettes. Mustard is the oldest known condiment. In 1853, Maurice Grey of Dijon, France, mechanized the processing of mustard seeds.

SALT, when used in moderation, is a great flavour enhancer. It brings out the best in most ingredients. Sea salt contains a wonderful array of elements that benefit the body: iron, magnesium, calcium, potassium, manganese, zinc, and iodine. Sea salt is about 20 percent less salty than iodized table salt and has a purer taste.

PEPPERCORNS add spice to salads and should be freshly ground to capture their full biting flavour. Peppercorns, red chili pepper flakes, cayenne, or hot pepper sauce all add gusto to your salad dressing.

FRESH HOT CHILI PEPPERS also provide heat. Know your varieties and remember that bigger is often milder, and smaller is usually hotter. When handling hot peppers, protect your skin from the heat. Be sure not to touch your face or eyes, and wash your hands well immediately after handling hot peppers, or wear rubber gloves.

CAJUN SPICE seasoning adds a wonderful spicy taste to salads with meat, poultry, or seafood. Cajun spice is a blend of chili powder, ground cumin, cayenne, garlic, and onion. Look for a brand that includes dehydrated vegetables (onion, green bell pepper, celery, garlic, and parsley).

INDIAN CURRY PASTE provides a smoother and more well-rounded flavour than curry powder and can be found in various degrees of heat. I like using mild yellow curry paste to avoid overpowering other ingredients.

FRESH GINGER is hot and spicy-sweet. It provides a delicate yet distinctive aroma. When buying fresh ginger, make sure the skin is smooth, not shrivelled. Ginger has strong anti-inflammatory properties and is known to improve circulation and aid in digestion.

HOISIN SAUCE is a thick, sweet sauce made from soybean paste, garlic, vinegar, sugar, and spices. It can be found in Asian markets and most supermarkets. Once the jar has been opened, store it in the refrigerator.

SOY SAUCE is a staple of Asian cuisines and comes in a wide range of flavours and intensities. Salty and sweet, soy sauce is wonderful in dressings.

Kitchen Equipment

Apart from some chopping, slicing, and dicing—combined with a bit of creative inspiration—salads are generally easy to prepare. Here is a list of equipment in my kitchen that I use every day.

KNIVES You'll need a good-quality, sharp, medium-sized chef's knife; a small paring knife; and a serrated knife for slicing ingredients such as tomatoes or bread. Always remember to keep your knives sharp and your senses sharper.

SALAD SPINNER A salad spinner is a lidded container with an inner colander-like basket. A spinner makes it easy to dry lettuce, other greens, and herbs.

CHOPPING BOARDS Keep two different cutting boards in the kitchen to prevent cross-contamination: one for raw meat, poultry, and seafood, and one for fruits and vegetables.

TONGS A good-quality pair of stainless steel tongs is indispensable in the kitchen. A must at the grill!

MICROPLANE GRATER The microplane grater is a slender piece of lightweight stainless steel with superfine grating slots that make it a powerful performer. You can grate everything from Parmesan to citrus rind to fresh ginger with hardly any pressure.

MANDOLIN A mandolin is a handheld kitchen tool that can slice, shred, and julienne vegetables or fruits. Different blades can be attached and adjusted for thickness. The Japanese plastic kind works well, if you don't want to invest in the more expensive European stainless steel variety.

GRILL PAN Stovetop grill pans have ridges that give a striking pattern of scoring on the food, like an outdoor barbecue. Because of their ridges, grill pans let air circulate under the food by lifting it up off the solid surface. The advantage of using a grill pan is that you won't have to step outside in the winter to tend to the barbecue.

Other equipment you'll need

- Blender or food processor
- Colander
- Collapsible steamer rack
- Garlic press
- Kitchen shears
- Measuring utensils
- Mixing bowls in various sizes
- Non-stick baking sheets
- Non-stick frying pans (buy a good-quality set)
- Pepper grinder
- Salad plates or bowls and platters of various sizes
- Salad servers
- Skewers
- Small and medium-sized whisks
- Vegetable peeler

Maple-Glazed Pecans
or Honey-Glazed Walnuts

• MAKES 1 CUP (250 ML) •

Sweet and crunchy with a hint of heat, glazed nuts
are a great addition to your salad.

INGREDIENTS

2   Tbsp (30 mL) pure maple syrup
1   Tbsp (15 mL) brown sugar
pinch of sea salt
pinch of cayenne pepper OR chili
     powder

1   cup (250 mL) pecan halves

1   Position a rack in the centre of the oven
    and preheat to 325°F (160°C). Combine
    maple syrup, brown sugar, salt, and cayenne
    pepper in a small bowl. Add pecans and toss
    well to coat. Spread on a rimmed baking sheet
    lined with parchment paper or foil. Toast
    for 10 to 15 minutes, or until nuts are golden
    and sugar is bubbling. Let cool completely
    on baking sheet. Break apart if necessary.
    Can be made ahead and stored in an airtight
    container for up to 2 weeks.

TIP To make honey-glazed walnuts, substitute
liquid honey for the maple syrup and walnut
halves for the pecans.

17

Basic Vinaigrette

*This multi-purpose vinaigrette can be used on any greens,
other vegetables, grains, or beans.*

INGREDIENTS

2 Tbsp (30 mL) vinegar (you can use
   red or white wine vinegar, sherry
   vinegar, balsamic vinegar, apple
   cider vinegar, or a combination
   of your favourite vinegar and
   citrus juice)
1 tsp (5 mL) Dijon, honey Dijon,
   or grainy Dijon mustard
⅓ cup (80 mL) extra virgin olive oil,
   grapeseed oil, or safflower oil
sea salt and freshly ground pepper

1 Combine vinegar and mustard in a small
   bowl. Gradually whisk in oil until well
   combined, and season with salt and pepper
   to taste. Or, in a glass jar with a tight-fitting
   lid, combine all ingredients, shake to blend,
   and store in refrigerator for up to 4 days.
   Before using, bring to room temperature and
   shake well.

Basic Creamy Dressing

Creamy and delicious, this dressing can be used on any greens or vegetables. For a blue-cheese dressing, add ½ cup (125 mL) crumbled Gorgonzola, Roquefort, or Stilton cheese.

INGREDIENTS

½ cup (125 mL) yogurt, buttermilk, or sour cream

2 Tbsp (30 mL) low-fat mayonnaise

2 Tbsp (30 mL) finely chopped fresh herbs (such as cilantro, mint, basil, parsley, or tarragon)

2 tsp (10 mL) apple cider vinegar or fresh lemon or orange juice

1 garlic clove, minced, OR 1 Tbsp (15 mL) minced shallot

sea salt and freshly ground pepper

1 Combine all ingredients in a small bowl and whisk to combine. Or, place all ingredients in a glass jar with a tight-fitting lid, shake to blend, and store in refrigerator for up to 2 days. Shake well before using.

Leafy Green Salads

Mixed Greens with Apples & Maple-Glazed Pecans

This salad is outstanding. Sweet maple pecans, crunchy apple, peppery arugula, and smooth, slightly bitter Belgian endive—an unbeatable combination!

INGREDIENTS

1 tsp (5 mL) Dijon mustard

2 Tbsp (30 mL) minced shallots

2 Tbsp (30 mL) balsamic vinegar

2 Tbsp (30 mL) pure maple syrup

½ cup (125 mL) extra virgin olive oil

sea salt and freshly ground pepper

1 head Boston lettuce, torn into pieces

1 bunch arugula or watercress, trimmed

3 Belgian endives, cut lengthwise into strips

2 apples, cored and diced (prepare just before serving, or toss with a little lemon juice to prevent browning)

½ cup (125 mL) maple-glazed pecans, coarsely chopped (see recipe page 17)

½ cup (125 mL) crumbled chèvre or feta (optional)

1 FOR THE VINAIGRETTE: combine mustard, shallots, vinegar, and maple syrup in a small bowl. Gradually whisk in oil until well combined. Season with salt and pepper to taste and set aside. If making ahead, cover and refrigerate for up to 4 days.

2 Just before serving, place lettuce, arugula, endives, and apples in a large serving bowl. Add vinaigrette and toss to coat. Sprinkle with maple-glazed pecans and chèvre (if using).

Mixed Greens with Blackberries, Honey-Glazed Walnuts & Feta

The combination of berries, sweet crunchy nuts, and tangy feta tastes just as good as it sounds and is very appealing to the eye. You can substitute raspberries, blueberries, or strawberries for the blackberries.

INGREDIENTS

2 Tbsp (30 mL) fresh orange juice

½ tsp (2 mL) orange zest

1 Tbsp (15 mL) liquid honey

1 Tbsp (15 mL) champagne vinegar, white wine vinegar, or apple cider vinegar

3 Tbsp (45 mL) extra virgin olive oil

1 Tbsp (15 mL) walnut oil or additional extra virgin olive oil

sea salt and freshly ground pepper

8 cups (2 L) assorted greens (such as Boston and red leaf lettuce, baby greens, and watercress)

2 cups (500 mL) blackberries

1 cup (250 mL) diced feta

½ cup (125 mL) honey-glazed walnuts, coarsely chopped (see recipe page 17)

1 FOR THE VINAIGRETTE: combine orange juice, orange zest, honey, and vinegar in a small bowl. Gradually whisk in olive oil and walnut oil until well combined, and season with salt and pepper to taste. Set aside. If making ahead, cover and refrigerate for up to 4 days.

2 Just before serving, place greens in a serving bowl and toss with vinaigrette. Add berries, feta, and honey-glazed walnuts. Toss gently to combine.

Food is sustenance, but it's sensuous too. It's about love. —RUTH GANGBAR

Mixed Greens with Pears, Blue Cheese & Walnuts

This is a favourite salad that I often serve to guests. Walnuts have a distinct flavour and crisp bite and contain healthy fats on par with olive oil. A superb salad to serve with a juicy steak!

INGREDIENTS

2 tsp (10 mL) honey Dijon mustard
2 Tbsp (30 mL) minced shallots
2 Tbsp (30 mL) fresh lemon juice
1 Tbsp (15 mL) apple cider vinegar
¼ cup (60 mL) extra virgin olive oil
sea salt and freshly ground pepper

4 cups (1 L) mixed baby greens
2 Belgian endives, halved lengthwise
   and cut into strips
1 bunch watercress, larger stems
   removed
2 firm but ripe pears, thinly sliced
   (prepare just before serving, or toss
   with a little lemon juice to prevent
   browning)
¾ cup (185 mL) crumbled blue cheese
¾ cup (185 mL) coarsely chopped
   toasted walnuts (see tip page 8)

1 FOR THE VINAIGRETTE: combine mustard, shallots, lemon juice, and vinegar in a small bowl. Gradually whisk in olive oil until well combined, and season with salt and pepper to taste. Set aside. If making ahead, cover and refrigerate for up to 4 days.

2 Just before serving, place baby greens, endives, and watercress in a large bowl and toss with just enough vinaigrette to coat (you may not need it all). To serve, divide the salad among 4 to 6 plates. Place pear slices overtop and sprinkle crumbled blue cheese and walnuts over each salad.

Strawberries & Field Greens with Chèvre

• 6 SERVINGS •

This is a delicious and colourful salad. Substitute raspberries or blackberries for the strawberries and you'll have an entirely different taste experience.

INGREDIENTS

2 tsp (10 mL) Russian-style or honey Dijon mustard

1 garlic clove, minced

1 Tbsp (15 mL) pure maple syrup

1 Tbsp (15 mL) raspberry vinegar

1 Tbsp (15 mL) balsamic vinegar

¼ cup (60 mL) extra virgin olive oil

sea salt and freshly ground pepper

8 cups (2 L) mixed field greens or baby greens

2 cups (500 mL) sliced strawberries

½ cup (125 mL) crumbled chèvre

⅓ cup (80 mL) chopped fresh mint (optional)

⅓ cup (80 mL) toasted pine nuts or slivered almonds (see tip page 8)

1 FOR THE VINAIGRETTE: combine mustard, garlic, maple syrup, and raspberry and balsamic vinegars in a small bowl. Gradually whisk in olive oil until well combined. Season with salt and pepper to taste and set aside. If making ahead, cover and refrigerate for up to 4 days.

2 Just before serving, combine field greens, strawberries, chèvre, mint (if using), and pine nuts in a large bowl. Toss gently with just enough vinaigrette to coat lightly (you may not need it all).

Herb & Berry Salad with Lemon Vinaigrette

In many Mediterranean countries, fresh herbs are used as primary salad ingredients. Enjoy this refreshing, versatile herb salad by experimenting with the berries, nuts, cheeses, and herbs of your choice. Buy the freshest ingredients you can find. Serve this salad "European style," after the main course, or arrange lamb chops or slices of grilled steak on top for a satisfying and stunning main-course salad.

INGREDIENTS

2 tsp (10 mL) grainy mustard or Dijon mustard

1 tsp (5 mL) liquid honey

⅓ cup (80 mL) fresh lemon juice

⅓ cup (80 mL) extra virgin olive oil freshly ground pepper

2 heads Boston or red leaf lettuce, torn into bite-sized pieces

½ cup (125 mL) torn fresh basil

½ cup (125 mL) coarsely chopped fresh parsley

½ cup (125 mL) chopped fresh cilantro

¼ cup (60 mL) chopped fresh mint

½ cup (125 mL) feta, chèvre, or blue cheese

½ cup (125 mL) berries (blackberries, strawberries, raspberries, or blueberries)

½ cup (125 mL) chopped toasted pecans, pistachios, or pine nuts (see tip page 8)

1 FOR THE VINAIGRETTE: combine mustard, honey, and lemon juice in a small bowl. Gradually whisk in olive oil until well combined, and season with pepper to taste. Set aside.

2 Just before serving, place lettuce, basil, parsley, cilantro, and mint in a large salad bowl. Toss with vinaigrette. Add cheese, berries, and nuts. Toss gently to coat. You can also divide the herb salad among 6 individual plates and top each with cheese, berries, and nuts.

Italian-Style Salad

Surprisingly easy! When pressed for time, you can whip up this salad in seconds. The secret to its success is in the quality of the ingredients. I was introduced to this salad by an Italian friend; he likes to serve his salad after the main course.

INGREDIENTS

2 Tbsp (30 mL) fresh lemon juice

1 Tbsp (15 mL) red wine vinegar or balsamic vinegar

⅓ cup (80 mL) extra virgin olive oil

sea salt and freshly ground pepper

6 cups (1.5 L) mixed baby greens, torn into bite-sized pieces

1 romaine heart, coarsely chopped

1 radicchio, quartered and thinly sliced

½ cup (125 mL) coarsely grated Parmigiano Reggiano, or more to taste

1 FOR THE VINAIGRETTE: combine lemon juice and vinegar in a small bowl. Gradually whisk in olive oil until well combined, and season with salt and pepper to taste. Set aside.

2 Just before serving, combine baby greens, romaine, and radicchio in a large serving bowl and toss with vinaigrette to coat. Gently toss in cheese, or place cheese in a small bowl and pass around the table.

Venetian-Style Salad

This is my version of a simple and delicious salad my husband and I enjoyed on holiday in the fascinating, romantic city of Venice. Use top-quality Italian Parmigiano Reggiano for great results.

INGREDIENTS

2   Tbsp (30 mL) fresh lemon juice
1   tsp (5 mL) lemon zest
1   Tbsp (15 mL) balsamic vinegar
1   garlic clove, minced
⅓   cup (80 mL) extra virgin olive oil
sea salt and freshly ground pepper

4   cups (1 L) field greens or baby
    greens
½   radicchio, torn into bite-sized pieces
1   bunch arugula, trimmed
½   fennel bulb, cored and sliced paper-
    thin (use a mandolin if you have one)
1   cup (250 mL) halved grape or cherry
    tomatoes
½   cup (125 mL) thinly sliced red onion
½   cup (125 mL) coarsely grated
    Parmigiano Reggiano, or more
    to taste

1   FOR THE VINAIGRETTE: combine lemon juice, lemon zest, vinegar, and garlic in a small bowl. Whisk in olive oil until well combined, and season with salt and pepper to taste. Set aside. If making ahead, cover and refrigerate for up to 4 days.

2   Just before serving, combine field greens, radicchio, arugula, fennel, tomatoes, and onion in a large bowl. Toss gently with just enough vinaigrette to coat (you may not need it all). Gently toss in cheese, or place cheese in a small bowl and pass around the table.

Nothing will benefit human health and increase the chances for survival of life on earth as much as the evolution to a vegetarian diet. —ALBERT EINSTEIN

Mediterranean Salad with Sourdough Croutons

This is a superb salad that your family and friends will find irresistible! I enjoy allowing everyone personal creativity at the table by passing the ingredients around separately in colourful bowls (with the romaine, red leaf, and radicchio in one bowl). I double up on the remaining ingredients, including the vinaigrette, to make sure there is enough to satisfy everyone's taste. You can add other ingredients, such as thinly sliced fennel, sliced radishes, sliced cucumber, quartered artichoke hearts, or thinly sliced red pepper. For a main-course salad, add a plate of sliced, barbecued chicken, beef, or seafood to your table.

INGREDIENTS

2 tsp (10 mL) Dijon mustard

1 large garlic clove, minced

2 Tbsp (30 mL) sherry vinegar or red wine vinegar

2 Tbsp (30 mL) fresh lemon juice

1 Tbsp (15 mL) chopped fresh oregano or basil

1 Tbsp (15 mL) chopped fresh mint

⅓ cup (80 mL) extra virgin olive oil

sea salt and freshly ground pepper

1 head of romaine, torn into bite-sized pieces

1 head red leaf lettuce, torn into bite-sized pieces

½ head radicchio, quartered and sliced into thin strips

1 cup (250 mL) halved grape or cherry tomatoes

½ cup (125 mL) thinly sliced red onion

½ cup (125 mL) pitted, sliced kalamata olives

½ cup (125 mL) crumbled feta

3 cups (750 mL) sourdough bread croutons (see tip page 9)

1 FOR THE VINAIGRETTE: combine mustard, garlic, vinegar, lemon juice, oregano, and mint in a small bowl. Gradually whisk in oil until well combined, and season with salt and pepper to taste. Set aside.

2 Just before serving, place salad ingredients and croutons in a serving bowl. Drizzle with vinaigrette and toss lightly to coat.

TIP You can prepare all vegetables in the morning or the day before and store them separately in airtight containers or Ziploc bags. The vinaigrette is best when made ahead; place it in a jar and refrigerate up to 1 week. Croutons can be made ahead and stored in an airtight container for up to 4 days.

Salade Verte à la Crème

• 4 TO 6 SERVINGS •

This was my mother's recipe and a family favourite when I was growing up. We often had this salad on special occasions. Originally it was made with real cream; this is a much lighter version, and equally delicious.

INGREDIENTS

1 cup (250 mL) low-fat sour cream
¼ cup (60 mL) fresh lemon juice
2 tsp (10 mL) sugar
sea salt and freshly ground pepper

1 head Boston lettuce, torn into bite-sized pieces
1 small head red leaf lettuce, torn into bite-sized pieces
3 green onions, finely chopped

1 FOR THE DRESSING: combine sour cream, lemon juice, and sugar in a small bowl. Season with salt and pepper to taste. Set aside.

2 Just before serving, combine lettuces and green onions in a serving bowl. Toss gently with just enough dressing to coat (you may not need it all).

TIP For a tzatziki dressing, add 1 garlic clove to the dressing and add thinly sliced cucumber and chopped fresh mint to the salad.

First we eat with our eyes, then our sense of smell kicks in. —SARA WAXMAN

Spinach Salad with Pineapple & Curried Cashews

I take great pleasure in making lunch for my daughter, granddaughter, and daughter-in-law. They love salads with fruit, nuts, and a sweet dressing. I created this recipe as a refreshing and light lunch, to be served with the Roasted Sweet Potato Soup from my other book, For the Love of Soup, *and warm naan bread.*

INGREDIENTS

- 1 Tbsp (15 mL) pure maple syrup
- 1 tsp (5 mL) mild Indian curry paste or powder
- ½ cup (125 mL) coarsely chopped cashews

- 1 tsp (5 mL) Dijon mustard
- 2 Tbsp (30 mL) apple cider vinegar or white wine vinegar
- 1 Tbsp (15 mL) fresh lemon juice
- 2 tsp (10 mL) pure maple syrup or liquid honey
- ¼ cup (60 mL) grapeseed or safflower oil
- sea salt and freshly ground pepper

- 6 cups (1.5 L) baby spinach
- 2 cups (500 mL) diced fresh pineapple
- 1 sweet red or yellow pepper, thinly sliced
- ½ cup (125 mL) thinly sliced red onion
- 2 Tbsp (30 mL) chopped fresh mint
- 2 Tbsp (30 mL) chopped fresh cilantro

1 Position oven rack in the centre of the oven. Preheat oven to 350°F (180°C).

2 Combine maple syrup and curry paste in a small bowl. Add chopped cashews and toss. Spread on a parchment paper-lined baking sheet. Bake for 8 to 10 minutes, or until nuts are crisp and fragrant. Set aside to cool. Break apart if necessary.

3 FOR THE VINAIGRETTE: combine mustard, vinegar, lemon juice, and maple syrup in a small bowl. Gradually whisk in oil until well combined. Season with salt and pepper to taste and set aside.

4 Just before serving, combine spinach, pineapple, red pepper, red onion, mint, cilantro, and cashews in a large serving bowl and toss with vinaigrette to coat.

Market Salad
with Hoisin Dressing

Add an authentic touch to your salad with this amazing, flavourful dressing made with hoisin, a kind of Asian barbecue sauce. Experiment by adding any vegetable you like to this salad. Wonderful with grilled salmon, chicken, or tofu!

INGREDIENTS

3 Tbsp (45 mL) grapeseed or safflower oil
1 Tbsp (15 mL) unseasoned rice
   wine vinegar
1 Tbsp (15 mL) hoisin sauce
1 Tbsp (15 mL) liquid honey
2 tsp (10 mL) toasted sesame oil
1 garlic clove, minced
¼ tsp (1 mL) chili pepper flakes,
   OR pinch of cayenne pepper

8 cups (2 L) baby spinach or
   mixed baby greens
1 cup (250 mL) cherry or grape
   tomatoes, halved
1 cup (250 mL) bean sprouts (optional)
2 small carrots, thinly sliced on the diagonal
½ cucumber, peeled and cubed
½ cup (125 mL) thinly sliced radishes
½ cup (125 mL) thinly sliced celery
½ cup (125 mL) thinly sliced water chestnuts
2 green onions, thinly sliced

1 FOR THE DRESSING: whisk together grapeseed oil, vinegar, hoisin sauce, honey, sesame oil, garlic, and chili pepper flakes in a small bowl. Set aside. If making ahead, cover and refrigerate for up to 4 days.

2 Just before serving, combine spinach, tomatoes, bean sprouts (if using), carrots, cucumber, radishes, celery, water chestnuts, and green onions in a serving bowl. Toss with just enough dressing to coat (you may not need it all).

Orange Spinach Salad

This delicious, healthy salad is all about flavour, texture, and colour. Feel free to substitute any baby greens for the spinach. For a main-course salad, top with grilled salmon or chicken.

INGREDIENTS

1 tsp (5 mL) Dijon mustard

1 garlic clove, minced

1 tsp (5 mL) orange zest

1 Tbsp (15 mL) balsamic vinegar

¼ cup (60 mL) grapeseed or safflower oil

1 tsp (5 mL) toasted sesame oil

sea salt and freshly ground pepper

6 cups (1.5 L) baby spinach

2 cups (500 mL) baby arugula

2 navel oranges, peeled and cut into sections (see tip page 5)

4 radishes, thinly sliced

3 green onions, thinly sliced

½ cup (125 mL) chopped fresh cilantro

1 FOR THE VINAIGRETTE: combine mustard, garlic, orange zest, and vinegar in a small bowl. Gradually whisk in grapeseed and sesame oils until well combined. Season with salt and pepper to taste and set aside. If making ahead, cover and refrigerate for up to 4 days.

2 Just before serving, place spinach, arugula, orange sections, radishes, green onions, and cilantro in a serving bowl. Toss with just enough vinaigrette to coat (you may not need it all).

Spinach Salad with Cheddar, Maple Bacon & Croutons

If you have never tried maple-flavoured bacon, you are in for a treat! Combined with a sharp cheddar cheese and croutons, it makes a delightful salad. Spinach is a good source of calcium, iron, folate, and potassium. For a vegetarian version of this salad, substitute toasted nuts for the bacon.

INGREDIENTS

6 slices maple-flavoured bacon

½ tsp (2 mL) Dijon mustard
1 Tbsp (15 mL) finely chopped shallot
1 Tbsp (15 mL) fresh lemon juice
3 Tbsp (45 mL) extra virgin olive oil
sea salt and freshly ground pepper

8 cups (2 L) baby spinach
2 cups (500 mL) sourdough croutons
(see tip page 9)
1 cup (250 mL) shredded sharp
cheddar cheese

1 Heat a skillet over medium heat and brown bacon slices on both sides until crisp. Transfer to paper towels. When cool enough to handle, crumble bacon and set aside.

2 FOR THE VINAIGRETTE: combine mustard, shallot, and lemon juice in a small bowl. Gradually whisk in olive oil until well combined, and season with salt and pepper to taste. Set aside. If making ahead, cover and refrigerate up to 4 days.

3 Just before serving, place spinach in a large serving bowl and toss with vinaigrette. Add croutons, bacon, and cheese. Toss gently to coat.

TIP *If you cannot find maple-flavoured bacon, use regular bacon and add 2 tsp (10 mL) of real maple syrup to the vinaigrette.*

Warm Portobello Mushrooms
with Spinach, Pine Nuts & Caramelized Shallots

Mushrooms have a rich, meaty flavour that makes them an ideal substitute for meat in vegetarian dishes. You can use an assortment of wild mushrooms instead of the portobello.

INGREDIENTS

4 to 5 medium-sized portobello
  mushrooms (see tip page 5)

¼ cup (60 mL) extra virgin olive oil
6 medium-sized shallots, thinly sliced
2 garlic cloves, finely chopped
2 tsp (10 mL) fresh thyme
sea salt and freshly ground pepper

3 Tbsp (45 mL) balsamic vinegar
2 tsp (10 mL) Dijon mustard

6 cups (1.5 L) baby spinach or
  baby greens
¼ cup (60 mL) toasted pine nuts
  (see tip page 8)
½ cup (125 mL) grated fresh
  Parmesan cheese

1 Remove the mushroom stems and discard. Remove gills on the underside of the mushroom caps by scraping them with the side of a spoon (they have a slightly bitter taste and exude black liquid when cooked). Cut mushroom caps in half and slice. Set aside.

2 Heat olive oil in a large skillet over medium heat. Add shallots and sauté for 3 to 4 minutes, or until golden brown. Add mushrooms, garlic, and thyme. Season with salt and pepper to taste. Sauté until mushrooms are soft, about 5 minutes.

3 Meanwhile, combine vinegar and mustard in a small bowl. Pour over mushrooms, and stir to coat. Remove from heat.

4 Add mushrooms and liquid to spinach and toss lightly. Divide among 4 plates and sprinkle with pine nuts and Parmesan. Serve immediately.

Arugula, Fennel & Fig Salad with Shaved Parmesan

• 4 SERVINGS •

Figs grow abundantly in the warm climate of the Mediterranean. The season for fresh figs extends from late summer to early fall. This attractive salad features them in a wonderful combination of flavours.

INGREDIENTS

6 cups (1.5 L) baby arugula

½ small fennel bulb, cored and sliced paper-thin (use a mandolin, if you have one)

4 to 6 fresh, ripe figs, quartered

3 Tbsp (45 mL) extra virgin olive oil

2 Tbsp (30 mL) fresh lemon juice

sea salt and freshly ground pepper

shaved Parmesan cheese

1 Divide arugula among 4 salad plates. Arrange fennel and figs decoratively over the arugula.

2 FOR THE VINAIGRETTE: whisk oil and lemon juice in a small bowl. Season with salt and pepper to taste.

3 Drizzle vinaigrette over salads and garnish with shaved Parmesan cheese.

TIP Store ripe figs in the refrigerator, but bring them to room temperature before serving.

Arugula Salad with Orange-Balsamic Vinaigrette

This is one of my favourite salads. It is simple, nutritious, and full of flavour. Use the best-quality imported aged Parmigiano Reggiano for great results. Adding shaved fennel or sliced roasted beets gives this salad another dimension!

INGREDIENTS

2 Tbsp (30 mL) balsamic vinegar

2 Tbsp (30 mL) fresh orange juice

1 tsp (5 mL) orange zest

1 garlic clove, minced

¼ cup (60 mL) extra virgin olive oil

sea salt and freshly ground pepper

8 cups (2 L) baby arugula or any mix of baby greens

½ cup (125 mL) grated fresh Parmigiano Reggiano

1 FOR THE VINAIGRETTE: combine balsamic vinegar, orange juice, orange zest, and garlic in a small bowl. Gradually whisk in oil until well combined, and season with salt and pepper to taste. Set aside. If making ahead, cover and refrigerate for up to 4 days.

2 Just before serving, place arugula in a large bowl and toss with vinaigrette. Add Parmigiano Reggiano and toss lightly to coat.

There is no love sincerer than the love of food. —GEORGE BERNARD SHAW

Mâche, Arugula & Pear Salad with Pomegranate Vinaigrette

This is a great festive salad, perfect for holiday entertaining. Pomegranate seeds give each mouthful a burst of refreshing flavour, and the reduced pomegranate juice adds a wonderful, concentrated taste to the vinaigrette. Mâche, also called lamb's lettuce, has a mild flavour and is excellent combined with arugula.

INGREDIENTS

½ cup (125 mL) unsweetened pomegranate juice

2 Tbsp (30 mL) finely chopped shallots
1 Tbsp (15 mL) unseasoned rice wine vinegar or apple cider vinegar
1 tsp (5 mL) pure maple syrup
¼ cup (60 mL) extra virgin olive oil
sea salt and freshly ground pepper

4 cups (1 L) mâche
4 cups (1 L) baby arugula
2 small firm but ripe pears, sliced thinly lengthwise (prepare just before serving)
½ cup (125 mL) diced feta
⅓ cup (80 mL) pomegranate seeds (see tip page 6)
⅓ cup (80 mL) toasted pine nuts (see tip page 8)

1 Place pomegranate juice in a small saucepan and bring to a boil. Lower heat and simmer, uncovered, until juice is reduced to 2 Tbsp (30 mL). Remove from heat and let cool slightly.

2 Combine shallots, vinegar, maple syrup, and pomegranate reduction in a small bowl. Gradually whisk in olive oil until well combined, and season with salt and pepper to taste. Set aside. If making ahead, cover and refrigerate for up to 4 days.

3 Just before serving, place mâche and arugula in a large bowl. Toss with vinaigrette to coat. Transfer greens to a large, shallow bowl or platter. Arrange pear slices in a row over the greens and sprinkle with feta, pomegranate seeds, and nuts.

Belgian Endive & Apple Salad with Creamy Maple Dressing

This is a lovely side salad that pairs well with pork or chicken. It is also wonderful topped with crumbled blue cheese. Apples are rich in pectin, a soluble fibre that helps lower cholesterol.

INGREDIENTS

- 2 Tbsp (30 mL) low-fat yogurt
- 2 Tbsp (30 mL) low-fat mayonnaise
- 2 Tbsp (30 mL) pure maple syrup
- 2 Tbsp (30 mL) apple cider vinegar
- 2 Tbsp (30 mL) minced shallots
- 1 tsp (5 mL) Dijon mustard
- sea salt and freshly ground pepper

- 2 Belgian endives, cut crosswise into rings
- 4 cups (1 L) mixed baby greens
- 2 apples, cored and cut into matchsticks (prepare just before serving)
- 1 cup (250 mL) thinly sliced celery
- ½ cup (125 mL) coarsely chopped toasted walnuts (see tip page 8)

1 FOR THE DRESSING: whisk together yogurt, mayonnaise, maple syrup, cider vinegar, shallots, and mustard in a small bowl. Season with salt and pepper to taste and set aside. If making ahead, cover and refrigerate for up to 2 days.

2 Just before serving, place endives, baby greens, apples, celery, and toasted walnuts in a serving bowl. Toss with enough dressing to coat (you may not need it all).

The act of putting into your mouth what the earth has grown is perhaps your most direct interaction with the earth. —FRANCES MOORE LAPPÉ

Belgian Endive Salad
with Warm Chèvre

Belgian endive has a delicate taste and great crunch. This salad makes a lovely starter for a luncheon or dinner party. Serve with freshly baked baguette or a loaf of country-style bread for spreading the cheese.

INGREDIENTS

1 egg
½ cup (125 mL) panko or dry breadcrumbs
¼ cup (60 mL) minced fresh flat-leaf parsley
¼ tsp (1 mL) sea salt
¼ tsp (1 mL) freshly ground pepper
one 10 oz log (300 g) chèvre (see tip)

1 Tbsp (15 mL) Dijon mustard
1 garlic clove, minced
1 Tbsp (15 mL) liquid honey
2 Tbsp (30 mL) champagne vinegar or
   white wine vinegar

¼ cup (60 mL) extra virgin olive oil
sea salt and freshly ground pepper

2 Tbsp (30 mL) extra virgin olive oil (for
   cooking chèvre)

3 Belgian endives, cut crosswise into rings
1 large head of red leaf lettuce, torn into
   bite-sized pieces
½ cup (125 mL) coarsely chopped toasted
   pecans (see tip page 8)

1. In a small bowl, whisk egg with a few drops of water. In a separate small bowl, combine breadcrumbs, parsley, salt, and pepper. Cut chèvre log into 12 slices. Dip cheese slices into egg, then into breadcrumb mixture, pressing to coat. Place on a parchment paper-lined dish. Set aside. The chèvre slices may be prepared up to 8 hours ahead, then covered and refrigerated.

2. FOR THE VINAIGRETTE: combine mustard, garlic, honey, and vinegar. Gradually whisk in the ¼ cup (60 mL) of oil until well combined, and season with salt and pepper to taste. Set aside. If making ahead, cover and refrigerate for up to 4 days.

3. In a non-stick skillet, heat the 2 Tbsp (30 mL) of oil over medium heat. Cook chèvre rounds, turning once, until crisp and golden, about 3 minutes. Place on paper towels.

4. In a large bowl, toss endives and lettuce with vinaigrette, then divide among 6 plates. Arrange 2 slices of warm cheese on top of each salad and sprinkle with toasted pecans.

TIP Cut the package of goat cheese open with kitchen scissors to avoid squishing the cheese. A knife is not the best tool for cutting soft cheese into neat circles; try dental floss or fine thread stretched taut between your hands. Look for panko breadcrumbs in the Asian section of your supermarket or at an Asian market.

Roasted Asparagus & Mixed Greens with Shaved Parmesan

This is a family favourite—especially in spring, when the asparagus is at its best. Roasting concentrates the flavour of asparagus.

INGREDIENTS

20 asparagus spears, trimmed

1 Tbsp (15 mL) extra virgin olive oil

pinch of sea salt

pinch of freshly ground pepper

2 Tbsp (30 mL) minced shallots

2 Tbsp (30 mL) sherry vinegar or
red wine vinegar

1 tsp (5 mL) liquid honey

¼ cup (60 mL) extra virgin olive oil

freshly ground pepper

2 romaine hearts, torn into bite-sized pieces

2 cups (500 mL) baby arugula

shaved Parmesan cheese

1 Position a rack in the centre of the oven and preheat oven to 400°F (200°C).

2 Place asparagus on a rimmed baking sheet. Drizzle with oil and season with salt and pepper. Roast for 4 to 5 minutes, or until tender-crisp. Remove from the oven and set aside.

3 FOR THE VINAIGRETTE: combine shallots, vinegar, and honey in a small bowl. Gradually whisk in olive oil until well combined. Season with pepper to taste and set aside. If making ahead, cover and refrigerate for up to 4 days.

4 Just before serving, place romaine and arugula in a large bowl. Drizzle with half the vinaigrette and toss to coat evenly.

5 Divide salad among 4 plates and top each plate with asparagus. Drizzle remaining vinaigrette over asparagus and garnish with shaved Parmesan to taste.

TIP To make Parmesan shavings, draw a vegetable peeler or small knife across a block of Parmesan to create thin curls.

Beet Salad with Apple, Feta & Pine Nuts

This colourful salad is perfect for a special occasion. Beets have a sweet taste and supply potassium, folate, and vitamin C. Roasting the beets in their skins helps them retain their flavour and moisture.

INGREDIENTS

4   medium-sized roasted beets
    (see tip page 6)

2   tsp (10 mL) Dijon or grainy mustard
2   Tbsp (30 mL) minced shallots
2   Tbsp (30 mL) sherry vinegar or
    red wine vinegar
1   Tbsp (15 mL) fresh lemon juice
⅓   cup (80 mL) extra virgin olive oil
sea salt and freshly ground pepper

1   romaine heart, torn into bite-sized pieces
4   Belgian endives, halved lengthwise and
    cut into strips
1   large apple, cored and thinly sliced
    (prepare just before serving, or toss with
    a little lemon juice to prevent browning)

½   cup (125 mL) crumbled feta
¼   cup (60 mL) toasted pine nuts (see tip
    page 8)

1 Cut roasted beets in half and slice. Place them in a large bowl and set aside.

2 FOR THE VINAIGRETTE: combine mustard, shallots, vinegar, and lemon juice in a small bowl. Gradually whisk in olive oil until well combined. Season with salt and pepper to taste and set aside. If making ahead, cover and refrigerate for up to 4 days.

3 Just before serving, place romaine, endives, and apple in a bowl and toss with half the vinaigrette. Add remaining vinaigrette to beets and toss.

4 Divide salad among 6 salad plates or bowls. Arrange beets, feta, and pine nuts decoratively on top.

Beet, Avocado & Grapefruit Salad

Convert non-beet-eaters into beet lovers with this tasty salad. Not only is it full of flavour, it is loaded with powerhouse ingredients that help guard against disease.

INGREDIENTS

4 medium-sized roasted beets (see tip page 6)

2 tsp (10 mL) grainy Dijon mustard
2 tsp (10 mL) liquid honey
2 Tbsp (30 mL) sherry vinegar or red wine vinegar
1 Tbsp (15 mL) raspberry vinegar
⅓ cup (80 mL) extra virgin olive oil
sea salt and freshly ground black pepper

1 romaine heart, torn into bite-sized pieces
4 cups (1 L) baby spinach
1 large pink grapefruit, cut into sections (see tip page 5)
1 large firm but ripe avocado, pitted, peeled, and sliced (see tip page 5; prepare just before serving, or sprinkle with a little lemon juice to prevent browning)
½ small sweet onion, thinly sliced
½ cup (125 mL) coarsely chopped toasted pecans (see tip page 8)

1 Cut roasted beets in half and slice. Set aside.

2 FOR THE VINAIGRETTE: combine mustard, honey, sherry vinegar, and raspberry vinegar in a small bowl. Gradually whisk in olive oil until well combined. Season with salt and pepper to taste and set aside. If making ahead, cover and refrigerate for up to 4 days.

3 Just before serving, combine romaine, spinach, grapefruit, avocado, and onion in a large salad bowl. Toss with vinaigrette. Add beets and pecans and toss gently to coat.

Beet & Avocado Salad with Mini Horseradish Croutons

This elegant and colourful salad is packed with vitamins. Roasting the beets brings out their sweetness and intensifies their depth of flavour. You can use an assortment of coloured beets (red, golden, purple, or candy-striped). A local farmers' market will have the best selection.

INGREDIENTS

4 medium-sized roasted beets
   (see tip page 6)

1 cup (250 mL) finely diced French
   or Italian bread, crusts removed
2 Tbsp (30 mL) bottled grated
   horseradish, squeezed dry
1 Tbsp (15 mL) extra virgin olive oil
1 Tbsp (15 mL) butter

2 tsp (10 mL) Dijon mustard
1 garlic clove, minced
2 Tbsp (30 mL) sherry vinegar or
   red wine vinegar

1 Tbsp (15 mL) fresh lemon juice
⅓ cup (80 mL) grapeseed or safflower oil
   sea salt and freshly ground pepper

8 cups (2 L) mixed baby greens
1 large ripe but firm avocado, pitted, peeled,
   and sliced (see tip page 5; prepare just
   before serving, or sprinkle with a little
   lemon juice to prevent browning)

1 Cut roasted beets in half and slice. Set aside.

2 Place diced bread in a separate bowl and toss with horseradish. Heat oil and butter in a skillet over medium heat. When hot, add bread mixture. Stir frequently and cook until the mini croutons are golden brown and crisp. Set aside to cool.

3 FOR THE VINAIGRETTE: combine mustard, garlic, vinegar, and lemon juice in a small bowl. Gradually whisk in oil until well combined. Season with salt and pepper to taste and set aside. If making ahead, cover and refrigerate for up to 4 days.

4 Just before serving, place baby greens in a serving bowl and toss with vinaigrette. Add beets, croutons, and avocado and toss lightly to coat.

Watercress & Fennel Salad with Honey-Lime Vinaigrette

This salad is simply delicious and very refreshing. Feel free to substitute arugula for the watercress. For a main-course salad, top with grilled or poached salmon.

INGREDIENTS

2 Tbsp (30 mL) fresh lime juice

1 Tbsp (15 mL) rice wine vinegar
   or apple cider vinegar

1 Tbsp (15 mL) liquid honey

¼ cup (60 mL) extra virgin olive oil

sea salt and freshly ground pepper

1 medium fennel bulb, cored and
   sliced paper-thin (use a mandolin,
   if you have one)

½ small red onion, finely sliced
   (optional)

2 bunches watercress, larger stems
   removed, about 4 cups (1 L)

2 Tbsp (30 mL) chopped fresh parsley

2 Tbsp (30 mL) chopped fresh mint

1 FOR THE VINAIGRETTE: combine lime juice, vinegar, and honey in a small bowl. Gradually whisk in olive oil until well combined, and season with salt and pepper to taste. Set aside. If making ahead, cover and refrigerate for up to 4 days.

2 Just before serving, combine fennel, red onion (if using), watercress, parsley, and mint in a medium-sized serving bowl. Toss gently with vinaigrette to coat.

Watercress & Radish Salad

When entertaining, I sometimes serve this simple, refreshing salad after the main course. If you don't like radishes, substitute thinly sliced celery or fennel.

INGREDIENTS

1 tsp (5 mL) Dijon mustard

1 Tbsp (15 mL) finely chopped shallot

2 Tbsp (30 mL) champagne vinegar or good-quality white wine vinager

¼ cup (60 mL) extra virgin olive oil

sea salt and freshly ground pepper

2 bunches watercress, larger stems removed

4 cups (1 L) mixed baby greens

6 radishes, thinly sliced

1 FOR THE VINAIGRETTE: combine mustard, shallot, and vinegar in a small bowl. Gradually whisk in olive oil until well combined, and season with salt and pepper to taste. Set aside. If making ahead, cover and refrigerate for up to 4 days.

2 Just before serving, combine watercress, baby greens, and radishes in a large bowl and toss with vinaigrette.

Let food be your medicine and medicine be your food. —HIPPOCRATES

Garden Vegetable Salads
(Hold the Lettuce)

Asparagus & Orange Salad	58
Asparagus & Pea Shoot Salad	59
Fresh Bean Salad with Caramelized Shallots & Hazelnuts	60
Avocado, Tomato & Cucumber Salad with Basil Vinaigrette	62
Tomato Cucumber Salad with Mint & Cilantro	63
Caprese Salad	64
Tuscan Bread, Tomato & Olive Salad	65
Fresh Mushroom Salad with Gremolata Vinaigrette	66
Marinated Beet Salad with Mint & Chèvre	67
Avocado Salad	68
Herbed Watermelon Salad with Feta	69
Grilled Eggplant Salad with Tomatoes & Mozzarella Cheese	70
Grilled Vegetable Platter	72
Carrot Salad with Figs & Sunflower Seeds	73
Cabbage Slaw with Creamy Peppercorn Dressing	74
Cabbage Slaw with Apples & Maple-Glazed Pecans	75
Tofu & Napa Cabbage Slaw with Sesame-Ginger Dressing	76
Charred Corn Salad	78
Curried Carrot-Apple Salad	80

Asparagus & Orange Salad

This simple and healthy salad adds colour and flavour to any meal. Asparagus contains no fat or cholesterol and has more folic acid per serving than any other vegetable, while oranges contain both vitamin C and bioflavonoids. The flavours in this salad are enhanced when it sits at room temperature for at least 30 minutes before serving.

INGREDIENTS

2   lb (1 kg) asparagus, trimmed

1   tsp (5 mL) grainy Dijon mustard
2   Tbsp (30 mL) finely chopped shallots
1   tsp (5 mL) orange zest
2   Tbsp (30 mL) fresh orange juice
2   Tbsp (30 mL) balsamic vinegar
2   Tbsp (30 mL) extra virgin olive oil
1   tsp (5 mL) toasted sesame oil
sea salt and freshly ground pepper

2   navel oranges, peeled and cut
    into sections (see tip page 5)
2   Tbsp (30 mL) toasted sesame
    seeds (see tip page 8)

1   Cook whole asparagus in a large skillet of boiling, salted water for 2 to 3 minutes, or until tender-crisp. Drain asparagus, rinse under cold water, and pat dry on paper towels. Place asparagus on a large serving platter.

2   FOR THE VINAIGRETTE: combine mustard, shallots, orange zest, orange juice, and vinegar in a small bowl. Gradually whisk in olive oil and sesame oil until well combined. Season with salt and pepper to taste and set aside. If making ahead, cover and refrigerate for up to 4 days.

3   Drizzle the vinaigrette over the asparagus and garnish with orange sections and toasted sesame seeds.

Asparagus & Pea Shoot Salad

Pea shoots are the tendrils and top leaves of the snow pea plant. You can find them in specialty food stores or in Asian markets. If they are unavailable, substitute mâche or spinach. For a main-course salad, top with chunks of warm grilled salmon or slices of chicken.

INGREDIENTS

1   lb (500 g) asparagus, trimmed
    (about 16 to 20 spears)

1   Tbsp (15 mL) unseasoned rice
    wine vinegar
1   Tbsp (15 mL) fresh lemon juice
2   tsp (10 mL) liquid honey
2   tsp (10 mL) low-sodium soy sauce
2   tsp (10 mL) toasted sesame oil

4   cups (1 L) pea shoots
1   sweet red pepper, thinly sliced
1   Tbsp (15 mL) toasted sesame
    seeds (see tip page 8)

1   Cook whole asparagus in a large skillet of boiling, salted water for 2 to 3 minutes, or until tender-crisp. Drain asparagus and rinse under cold water. Pat dry on paper towels and set aside.

2   FOR THE DRESSING: whisk together rice wine vinegar, lemon juice, honey, soy sauce, and sesame oil in a small bowl. Set aside.

3   Place pea shoots on a medium-sized platter or on individual plates. Arrange asparagus and red pepper over the pea shoots and drizzle with dressing. Sprinkle with toasted sesame seeds.

Fresh Bean Salad with Caramelized Shallots & Hazelnuts

If you are lucky enough to find French haricots verts, use them in this salad. Hazelnuts can be replaced with toasted, slivered almonds or pine nuts.

INGREDIENTS

½ lb (250 g) green beans, trimmed

½ lb (250 g) yellow beans, trimmed

1 Tbsp (15 mL) extra virgin olive oil

4 to 6 shallots, thinly sliced

1 tsp (5 mL) Dijon mustard

2 tsp (10 mL) sherry vinegar or red wine vinegar

2 tsp (10 mL) fresh lemon juice

1 Tbsp (15 mL) extra virgin olive oil

sea salt and freshly ground pepper

⅓ cup (80 mL) toasted, skinned, and chopped hazelnuts (see tip)

1. Place green and yellow beans in a saucepan of boiling, salted water and cook for 3 to 4 minutes, or until tender-crisp. Drain and refresh under cold water. Pat dry with paper towels and place in a large bowl.

2. To caramelize shallots: heat olive oil in a small skillet over medium heat. Add sliced shallots and cook, stirring frequently, for about 6 minutes, or until golden brown. Remove from heat and set aside.

3. FOR THE VINAIGRETTE: combine mustard, vinegar, and lemon juice in a small bowl. Gradually whisk in oil until well combined. Season with salt and pepper to taste and set aside. If making ahead, cover and refrigerate for up to 4 days.

4. Add shallots, vinaigrette, and hazelnuts to beans. Adjust seasonings and toss to coat. This salad is best served warm or at room temperature.

TIP Toast hazelnuts in a 350°F (180°C) oven in a shallow baking pan for 5 to 7 minutes, until lightly browned and fragrant. Rub the warm hazelnuts in a kitchen towel to remove skins.

Avocado, Tomato & Cucumber Salad with Basil Vinaigrette

This is a simple and delicious side salad that pairs well with any meat, chicken, or fish. If regular tomatoes are not at their best, use cherry or grape tomatoes instead. Avocados are loaded with vitamins, minerals, and essential fatty acids. In small doses, they are one of nature's most nutritious gifts.

INGREDIENTS

½ cup (125 mL) lightly packed fresh basil

2 Tbsp (30 mL) balsamic vinegar

¼ tsp (1 mL) sea salt

¼ tsp (1 mL) freshly ground pepper

3 Tbsp (45 mL) extra virgin olive oil

2 ripe but firm avocados, pitted, peeled, and sliced (see tip page 5; prepare just before serving, or drizzle with a little lemon juice to prevent browning)

2 tomatoes, cut in wedges

1 English cucumber, cut in half lengthwise and sliced

½ cup (125 mL) thinly sliced red or green onions (optional)

1 FOR THE VINAIGRETTE: in a food processor, purée basil with vinegar, salt, and pepper, then blend in oil. (If you don't have a food processor, chop basil leaves finely and pound to a paste with the salt before mixing with the rest of the ingredients.) Set aside.

2 Place avocado slices on 1 side of a serving platter, tomato slices in the centre, and cucumber slices on the other side. Sprinkle onions on top of salad (if using). Drizzle with basil vinaigrette.

Tomato Cucumber Salad
with Mint & Cilantro

• 4 TO 6 SERVINGS •

*This is a delicious, refreshing summer side salad that is very easy
to prepare. Tomatoes contain lycopene, an antioxidant that helps
in the fight against certain cancers and diseases.*

INGREDIENTS

3   ripe field tomatoes, cut into wedges
1   English cucumber, peeled, halved
    lengthwise, and thinly sliced
½   cup (125 mL) thinly sliced red onion
2   Tbsp (30 mL) chopped fresh mint
2   Tbsp (30 mL) chopped fresh cilantro
½   cup (125 mL) crumbled feta
    (optional)

2   Tbsp (30 mL) sherry vinegar or
    red wine vinegar
1   Tbsp (15 mL) fresh lemon juice
1   garlic clove, minced
¼   cup (60 mL) extra virgin olive oil
sea salt and freshly ground pepper

1   Arrange tomatoes, cucumber, and red onion
    decoratively on a large platter. Sprinkle with
    mint, cilantro, and feta (if using).

2   FOR THE VINAIGRETTE: combine vinegar,
    lemon juice, and garlic in a small bowl.
    Gradually whisk in olive oil until well com-
    bined. Season with salt and pepper to taste.

3   Drizzle vinaigrette over the salad and serve
    immediately.

63

Caprese Salad

Make this delicious Italian classic in the summertime, when tomatoes are at their peak. Buffalo mozzarella is made from the milk of water buffalos; soft and spongy, it is considered the best mozzarella. It is sold, packed in liquid, at well-stocked supermarkets and in cheese shops.

INGREDIENTS

4 medium-ripe field tomatoes, sliced
2 buffalo mozzarella balls, sliced
sea salt and freshly ground pepper

3 Tbsp (45 mL) extra virgin olive oil
2 Tbsp (30 mL) balsamic vinegar
¼ cup (60 mL) torn fresh basil

1 On a large platter, alternate tomato slices and mozzarella slices, slightly overlapping them. Season with salt and pepper to taste.

2 Drizzle olive oil and balsamic vinegar over the salad and garnish with basil. Serve at room temperature.

TIP Instead of buffalo mozzarella, you can substitute bocconcini cheese. It is also sold packed in liquid and is easier to find and less expensive. If using bocconcini, slice it and scatter over the sliced tomatoes.

Tuscan Bread, Tomato & Olive Salad

• 4 TO 6 SERVINGS •

I was first introduced to this Italian salad on a walking trip in Tuscany with my husband and a group of great friends. Every day, the tour guides had a picnic lunch prepared for us at the top of a mountain. We feasted our eyes on magnificent vistas and savoured our superb lunch. For a main-course salad, add thin strips of grilled chicken, chunks of tuna, or cooked cannellini beans.

INGREDIENTS

1 tsp (5 mL) Dijon mustard

2 garlic cloves, minced

2 Tbsp (30 mL) balsamic, sherry, or red wine vinegar

2 Tbsp (30 mL) fresh lemon juice

2 Tbsp (30 mL) extra virgin olive oil

sea salt and freshly ground pepper

4 ripe field tomatoes, cored, seeded, and diced (see tip below)

½ small sweet onion, thinly sliced

½ English cucumber, peeled and diced (optional)

¾ cup (185 mL) pitted dry-cured black olives, chopped

3 Tbsp (45 mL) chopped fresh basil

3 Tbsp (45 mL) chopped fresh mint

4 cups (1 L) ciabatta bread or Italian bread croutons (see tip page 9)

1 FOR THE VINAIGRETTE: combine mustard, garlic, vinegar, and lemon juice in a serving bowl. Gradually whisk in olive oil until well combined, and season with salt and pepper to taste.

2 Just before serving, add tomatoes, onion, cucumber (if using), olives, basil, and mint to the vinaigrette. Gently toss in toasted bread cubes.

TIP To seed tomatoes, cut in half and gently squeeze seeds from each half.

Fresh Mushroom Salad with Gremolata Vinaigrette

• 4 SERVINGS •

Gremolata is a mixture of parsley, lemon zest, and garlic. Parsley is one of the richest food sources of vitamin C. Here, it combines delightfully with lemony vinaigrette, mushrooms, and Parmesan cheese.

INGREDIENTS

1 tsp (5 mL) Dijon mustard

1 garlic clove, minced

1 tsp (5 mL) lemon zest

2 Tbsp (30 mL) fresh lemon juice

2 Tbsp (30 mL) extra virgin olive oil

sea salt and freshly ground pepper

½ lb (250 g) medium-sized button mushrooms

½ cup (125 mL) coarsely chopped flat-leaf parsley

⅓ cup (80 mL) coarsely grated fresh Parmesan cheese

1 FOR THE VINAIGRETTE: combine mustard, garlic, lemon zest, and lemon juice in a small bowl. Gradually whisk in olive oil until well combined, and season with salt and pepper to taste. Set aside. If making ahead, cover and refrigerate for up to 4 days.

2 Just before serving, trim and wash mushrooms under running cold water; dry immediately using paper towels. Avoid submerging mushrooms in water. Slice mushrooms thinly and place them in a serving bowl. Toss with vinaigrette, parsley, and cheese.

Marinated Beet Salad with Mint & Chèvre

The vinaigrette permeates the beets and gives them a wonderful sweet-and-sour flavour after marinating for a few hours. They are a brilliant side dish to just about anything.

INGREDIENTS

8 medium-sized roasted beets (see tip page 6)

¼ cup (60 mL) fresh lemon juice OR balsamic vinegar

¼ cup (60 mL) extra virgin olive oil

2 Tbsp (30 mL) finely chopped red onion

1 Tbsp (15 mL) liquid honey

sea salt and freshly ground pepper

⅓ cup (80 mL) chopped fresh mint

1 Cut the roasted beets in half and slice thinly. Place in a large bowl and set aside.

2 FOR THE VINAIGRETTE: whisk together vinegar, oil, onion, and honey in a small bowl. Season with salt and pepper to taste.

3 Add vinaigrette to beets, cover, and refrigerate for at least 1 hour. If making ahead, cover and refrigerate up to 3 days.

4 Just before serving, place beets in a serving bowl or on a platter and sprinkle mint and chèvre over the salad.

Happiness is when what you think, what you say, and what you do are in harmony.
—MAHATMA GANDHI

Avocado Salad

This salad makes a simple, splendid side dish. Avocados contain heart-healthy monounsaturated fat and no sodium, cholesterol, or trans fats. One avocado tree can produce about 500 avocados a year—that's 200 pounds (91 kg) of fruit.

INGREDIENTS

3 Tbsp (45 mL) fresh lemon juice
2 Tbsp (30 mL) extra virgin olive oil
1 tsp (5 mL) Worcestershire sauce
sea salt and freshly ground pepper

4 medium-sized Boston lettuce leaves
2 or 3 ripe but firm avocados, pitted, peeled, and sliced (see tip page 5; prepare just before serving)
½ small red onion, thinly sliced
½ cup (125 mL) chopped fresh flat-leaf parsley or cilantro

1 FOR THE DRESSING: whisk together lemon juice, olive oil, and Worcestershire sauce in a small bowl. Season with salt and pepper to taste and set aside.

2 Place lettuce leaves on a large plate or on individual plates. Top each leaf with sliced avocado and red onion. Drizzle dressing overtop and garnish with parsley.

Happiness often sneaks in through a door you didn't know you left open. —**JOHN BARRYMORE**

Herbed Watermelon Salad
with Feta

This light, refreshing, and colourful salad has become a favourite with my family and friends. Serve in individual glass bowls or in a lettuce leaf for a beautiful presentation. This salad is a fantastic summertime side dish; it can also be topped with brochettes of grilled shrimp for a main-course salad.

INGREDIENTS

6 cups (1.5 L) cubed seedless watermelon

1 cup (250 mL) peeled, finely chopped cucumber

½ cup (125 mL) finely chopped sweet yellow or red pepper

½ cup (125 mL) sliced black olives

⅓ cup (80 mL) finely chopped red onion

1 jalapeño pepper, seeded and finely chopped

⅓ cup (80 mL) chopped fresh cilantro

⅓ cup (80 mL) chopped fresh mint

2 Tbsp (30 mL) chopped fresh basil

3 Tbsp (45 mL) fresh lime juice

1 tsp (5 mL) lime zest

2 Tbsp (30 mL) extra virgin olive oil

1 Tbsp (15 mL) liquid honey

sea salt

1 cup (250 mL) diced feta

1 Place watermelon, cucumber, yellow pepper, olives, red onion, jalapeño, cilantro, mint, and basil in a large bowl.

2 FOR THE VINAIGRETTE: whisk together lime juice, lime zest, olive oil, and honey in a small bowl. Season with salt to taste and set aside.

3 Just before serving, drain excess liquid from watermelon mixture, then add vinaigrette and feta to the salad and toss lightly to coat.

TIP *This salad can be made 1 or 2 hours before serving, but keep in mind that the watermelon and cucumber will release their juices and make the salad a little watery. If making ahead, cover and refrigerate until ready to use, and drain some of the juices before serving.*

Grilled Eggplant Salad with Tomatoes & Mozzarella Cheese

Eggplant contains fibre, iron, potassium, vitamin K, and chlorogenic acid, a cancer-fighting antioxidant. Make this an exceptionally superb and satisfying dish by topping the salad with pieces of grilled fish or chicken.

INGREDIENTS

1   Tbsp (15 mL) fresh lemon juice
1   Tbsp (15 mL) balsamic vinegar
1   large garlic clove, minced
2   Tbsp (30 mL) extra virgin olive oil
sea salt and freshly ground pepper

1   medium eggplant
extra virgin olive oil for brushing
sea salt and freshly ground pepper

3   tomatoes, sliced
1   large buffalo mozzarella ball, sliced,
    OR 6 bocconcini balls, quartered
½   cup (125 mL) thinly sliced red onion
¼   cup (60 mL) coarsely chopped fresh
      basil or oregano
¼   cup (60 mL) chopped kalamata olives

1   FOR THE VINAIGRETTE: combine lemon juice, vinegar, and garlic in a small bowl. Gradually whisk in olive oil until well combined, and season with salt and pepper to taste. Set aside. If making ahead, cover and refrigerate up to 4 days.

2   Preheat a barbecue, indoor grill, or grill pan to medium-high.

3   Cut eggplant into ½-inch (1 cm) slices, brush both sides of each slice with olive oil, and season lightly with salt and pepper. Place eggplant slices on the grill (if using a grill pan, you will need to grill in batches) and brown on both sides for 3 to 4 minutes per side or until tender.

4   Remove eggplant from the barbecue or grill and arrange decoratively on a medium-sized platter. Top with alternating slices of tomato and mozzarella. (If using bocconcini, scatter it on top of tomatoes.) Drizzle with the vinaigrette. Arrange red onion, basil, and olives on top. Serve immediately.

TIP Buffalo mozzarella and bocconcini are balls of fresh cheese, sold packed in water or whey (see page 64). You can substitute with feta.

Grilled Vegetable Platter

Grilled vegetables are scrumptious and easy to prepare. The vegetables caramelize when roasting, releasing their sweet essence. This makes a great side dish, a substantial first course, or a vegetarian main dish. You can add other vegetables, such as asparagus, mushrooms, and tomatoes. Serve while the vegetables are warm, or at room temperature.

INGREDIENTS

¼ cup (60 mL) extra virgin olive oil

2 garlic cloves, minced

½ tsp (2 mL) sea salt

½ tsp (2 mL) freshly ground pepper

3 sweet red or yellow peppers, quartered and seeded

2 Japanese eggplants, cut in half lengthwise

2 zucchini, cut in half lengthwise

1 large sweet onion, sliced in ½-inch (1 cm) rounds

1 cup (250 mL) diced feta

3 Tbsp (45 mL) chopped fresh parsley

2 Tbsp (30 mL) chopped fresh mint or basil

3 Tbsp (45 mL) balsamic vinegar

1 Whisk together olive oil, garlic, salt, and pepper in a small bowl.

2 Preheat barbecue grill to medium-high heat. Brush vegetables with oil mixture and place on the grill. Grill for 3 to 4 minutes per side, or until vegetables are tender-crisp. Remove to a large platter. When cool enough to handle, slice vegetables into bite-sized pieces and arrange on a large platter.

3 Sprinkle feta, parsley, and mint over the vegetables and drizzle with balsamic vinegar.

Carrot Salad with Figs & Sunflower Seeds

• 4 TO 6 SERVINGS •

This is a wonderful side dish with grilled pork chops or chicken. Carrots are one of the richest sources of beta carotene. Your best guarantee of freshness is to buy carrots in bunches, with their leafy green tops still attached. You can substitute raisins, cranberries, or dates for the figs.

INGREDIENTS

⅓ cup (80 mL) fresh orange juice

1 tsp (5 mL) orange zest

1 Tbsp (15 mL) apple cider vinegar

1 Tbsp (15 mL) extra virgin olive oil

1 Tbsp (15 mL) walnut oil or additional extra virgin olive oil

sea salt and freshly ground pepper

4 cups (1 L) peeled and coarsely grated carrots

6 to 8 dried figs, chopped

½ cup (125 mL) sunflower seeds or coarsely chopped peanuts

2 green onions, finely chopped

2 Tbsp (30 mL) chopped fresh flat-leaf parsley or cilantro

1 FOR THE VINAIGRETTE: combine orange juice, orange zest, and vinegar in a large bowl. Gradually whisk in olive and walnut oils until well combined, and season with salt and pepper to taste. Set aside.

2 Add carrots, figs, sunflower seeds, green onions, and parsley to the vinaigrette and toss to combine. If making ahead, cover and refrigerate until ready to serve.

Here is a test to find whether your mission on earth is finished: if you're alive, it isn't.
—RICHARD BACH

Cabbage Slaw with Creamy Peppercorn Dressing

• 6 TO 8 SERVINGS •

This delicious cabbage slaw is a wonderful accompaniment to almost any meal. My family loves it with burgers or sandwiches, or with grilled meats or fish. Cabbage is an excellent source of vitamin C, high in folate and potassium, and a good source of fibre.

INGREDIENTS

½ cup (125 mL) buttermilk, low-fat sour cream, or yogurt

3 Tbsp (45 mL) low-fat mayonnaise

2 Tbsp (30 mL) fresh lemon juice

2 Tbsp (30 mL) apple cider vinegar

1 Tbsp (15 mL) liquid honey

1 garlic clove, minced

1 tsp (5 mL) Dijon mustard

¼ tsp (1 mL) freshly ground pepper

sea salt

8 cups (2 L) shredded Savoy cabbage (about 1 medium-sized head)

1 cup (250 mL) finely chopped sweet onion

1 cup (250 mL) finely chopped celery

1 cup (250 mL) finely chopped carrots

½ cup (125 mL) chopped fresh flat-leaf parsley

1 FOR THE DRESSING: whisk together buttermilk, mayonnaise, lemon juice, vinegar, honey, garlic, mustard, and pepper in a large bowl. Season with salt to taste.

2 Add cabbage, onion, celery, carrots, and parsley to the dressing and toss to combine. If making ahead, cover and refrigerate up to 2 days.

Cabbage Slaw with Apples & Maple-Glazed Pecans

This colourful, crunchy side salad is wonderful with turkey at Thanksgiving or Christmas, or with any other holiday meal. It would make a nice accompaniment to a barbecue during the warmer months, too. If making ahead, hold off on adding the pecans until just before serving to maintain their crunch.

INGREDIENTS

- 1 tsp (5 mL) Dijon mustard
- 2 Tbsp (30 mL) apple cider vinegar
- 1 Tbsp (15 mL) pure maple syrup
- 2 Tbsp (30 mL) grapeseed or safflower oil
- sea salt and freshly ground pepper

- 3 cups (750 mL) thinly sliced red cabbage
- 3 cups (750 mL) thinly sliced napa or Savoy cabbage
- 2 small Granny Smith apples, cored and diced (prepare just before serving, or sprinkle with a little lemon juice to prevent browning)
- ½ cup (125 mL) dried cranberries
- 1 cup (250 mL) maple-glazed pecans, coarsely chopped (see recipe page 17)

1 FOR THE VINAIGRETTE: combine mustard, vinegar, and maple syrup in a small bowl. Gradually whisk in oil until well combined, and season with salt and pepper to taste. Set aside.

2 Place red and napa cabbages, apples, cranberries, and chopped pecans in a large bowl, and toss with vinaigrette.

TIP You could use a food processor or mandolin to thinly slice the cabbage.

Tofu & Napa Cabbage Slaw with Sesame-Ginger Dressing

This crunchy slaw is satisfying and scrumptious. The best thing about tofu—besides its nutritional value—is the way it absorbs flavours. Here, it is served warm on top of the salad.

INGREDIENTS

2 garlic cloves, minced

1 Tbsp (15 mL) grated fresh ginger

2 Tbsp (30 mL) unseasoned rice wine vinegar

2 Tbsp (30 mL) fresh lemon juice

1 Tbsp (15 mL) low-sodium soy sauce

2 tsp (10 mL) honey OR maple syrup

¼ cup (60 mL) grapeseed or safflower oil

2 tsp (10 mL) toasted sesame oil

freshly ground pepper

6 cups (1.5 L) shredded napa cabbage

two 10 oz (284 mL) cans mandarin oranges, drained

6 to 8 small radishes, cut in half and thinly sliced

2 medium-sized carrots, coarsely grated

3 green onions, thinly sliced

½ cup (125 mL) chopped fresh cilantro or flat-leaf parsley

¾ cup (185 mL) coarsely chopped peanuts or cashews

1 package (12 oz/350 g) extra-firm tofu, cut into bite-sized cubes

1 FOR THE DRESSING: combine garlic, ginger, vinegar, lemon juice, soy sauce, and honey in a small bowl. Gradually whisk in grapeseed and sesame oils until well combined. Season generously with pepper. Set aside. If making ahead, cover and refrigerate for up to 4 days.

2 Combine napa cabbage, mandarin oranges, radishes, carrots, green onions, cilantro, and peanuts in a large bowl. Set aside.

3 Place tofu and 2 Tbsp (30 mL) of the dressing in a large non-stick skillet. Sauté over medium-high heat until golden, about 10 minutes. Remove from heat.

4 Meanwhile, toss salad with remaining dressing and place on a large platter or on individual plates. Serve salad topped with warm tofu.

TIP You can prepare all vegetables in the morning or the day before and store them in an airtight container or Ziploc bag. Add peanuts just before serving to maintain their crunch.

Charred Corn Salad

The distinctive combination of fresh ginger, lime, cilantro, and mint lends a burst of flavour to this perfect side-dish salad. Technically, corn is not a vegetable but a grain; like other whole grains, it is a good source of dietary fibre, and is digested more slowly than refined grains. Make the salad ahead to give the flavours time to blend, but hold off on adding the avocado until ready to serve.

INGREDIENTS

4 cobs fresh corn
extra virgin olive oil for brushing

1 large garlic clove, minced
1 tsp (5 mL) grated fresh ginger
2 Tbsp (30 mL) fresh lime juice
1 Tbsp (15 mL) apple cider vinegar
1 tsp (5 mL) liquid honey
2 Tbsp (30 mL) extra virgin olive oil
sea salt and freshly ground pepper

1 sweet red or orange pepper, diced
1 firm but ripe avocado, pitted, peeled, and chopped (see tip page 5; prepare just before serving)
1 jalapeño pepper, seeded and finely chopped
2 green onions, finely chopped
2 Tbsp (30 mL) chopped fresh cilantro or flat-leaf parsley
1 Tbsp (15 mL) chopped fresh mint

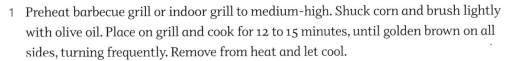

1 Preheat barbecue grill or indoor grill to medium-high. Shuck corn and brush lightly with olive oil. Place on grill and cook for 12 to 15 minutes, until golden brown on all sides, turning frequently. Remove from heat and let cool.

2 FOR THE DRESSING: combine garlic, ginger, lime juice, vinegar, and honey in a large serving bowl. Gradually whisk in olive oil until well combined, and season with salt and pepper to taste. Set aside.

3 Scrape kernels off corn cobs with a serrated knife and add to the dressing.

4 Add red pepper, avocado, jalapeño, green onions, cilantro, and mint to the corn. Toss to combine. Serve at room temperature or chilled.

TIP Choose fresh corn that is bright yellow, with firm kernels. Use fresh corn within 1 or 2 days of purchase.

Curried Carrot-Apple Salad

This is a wonderful side dish for meat, poultry, or seafood. Buy carrots in bunches, with their leafy green tops still attached. Use a mandolin, if you have one, to julienne the carrots.

INGREDIENTS

2 Tbsp (30 mL) low-fat sour cream or yogurt

2 Tbsp (30 mL) low-fat mayonnaise

2 Tbsp (30 mL) fresh lime juice

1 Tbsp (15 mL) liquid honey

1 tsp (5 mL) curry paste or powder

sea salt and freshly ground pepper

4 cups (1 L) julienne carrots (cut in very thin matchsticks)

1 Granny Smith apple, cored and finely chopped (prepare just before serving, or sprinkle with a little lemon juice to prevent browning)

¼ cup (60 mL) chopped fresh cilantro or flat-leaf parsley

½ cup (125 mL) dried cranberries

1 FOR THE DRESSING: whisk together sour cream, mayonnaise, lime juice, honey, and curry paste in a small bowl. Season with salt and pepper to taste and set aside. If making ahead, cover and refrigerate up to 2 days.

2 Combine carrots, apple, cilantro, and cranberries in a large bowl. Toss with dressing.

Fennel & Carrot Salad

This refreshing salad with its satisfying crunch is good any time of the year, with any main-course dish. It is a quick-fix salad if you use a mandolin to julienne the fennel and carrots. A food processor with a large shredding blade will also do the job.

INGREDIENTS

½ cup (125 mL) fresh orange juice

1 Tbsp (15 mL) balsamic vinegar

1 Tbsp (15 mL) fresh lemon juice

½ tsp (2 mL) sugar

¼ tsp (1 mL) chili pepper flakes, or to taste

2 Tbsp (30 mL) extra virgin olive oil

sea salt and freshly ground pepper

1 medium fennel bulb, trimmed, halved lengthwise, cored, and julienne

3 to 4 medium carrots, julienne or coarsely shredded

2 Tbsp (30 mL) finely chopped green onions

2 Tbsp (30 mL) chopped fresh mint

2 Tbsp (30 mL) chopped fresh flat-leaf parsley or cilantro

1 FOR THE VINAIGRETTE: combine orange juice, vinegar, lemon juice, sugar, and chili pepper flakes in a large bowl. Gradually whisk in olive oil until well combined, and season with salt and pepper to taste.

2 Add fennel, carrots, green onions, mint, and parsley to the vinaigrette and toss to coat.

Fennel & Orange Salad

Crunchy licorice-flavoured fennel, sweet and juicy orange, and the lively bite of red onion combine to make an incredibly refreshing treat that complements spicy foods perfectly. You can add roasted beets for extra goodness or avocado for luxurious silkiness.

INGREDIENTS

2   Tbsp (30 mL) fresh lemon juice

1   tsp (5 mL) lemon zest

2   Tbsp (30 mL) extra virgin olive oil

sea salt and freshly ground pepper

1   large fennel bulb, halved lengthwise, cored and sliced paper-thin (use a mandolin if you have one), some fronds reserved for garnish

2   navel oranges, peeled and cut into sections (see tip page 5)

½   small red onion, thinly sliced

2   Tbsp (30 mL) chopped fresh flat-leaf parsley

1   FOR THE VINAIGRETTE: combine lemon juice and zest in a small bowl. Whisk in olive oil until well combined, and season with salt and pepper to taste. Set aside.

2   Combine fennel, oranges, onion, and parsley in a medium-sized serving bowl and toss with vinaigrette to coat. Garnish with fennel fronds.

Roasted Sweet Pepper Salad

This is a lovely side dish! Roast lots of peppers when they are at their best so that you can enjoy them through the fall and winter months. Once roasted, peppers freeze very well. Don't forget to enjoy them in soup as well: try the Roasted Red Pepper Soup in my previous cookbook, For the Love of Soup.

INGREDIENTS

4 sweet red peppers, roasted (see tip page 6)

4 sweet yellow or orange peppers, roasted (see tip page 6)

¼ cup (60 mL) kalamata olives, seeded and chopped

¼ cup (60 mL) chopped fresh flat-leaf parsley

1 large garlic clove, minced

1 Tbsp (15 mL) sherry vinegar or red wine vinegar

2 Tbsp (30 mL) extra virgin olive oil

freshly ground pepper

1 Cut roasted peppers into thin strips and place them in a medium-sized bowl along with the olives.

2 FOR THE VINAIGRETTE: combine parsley, garlic, and vinegar in a small bowl. Gradually whisk in olive oil until well combined. Season with pepper to taste.

3 Add vinaigrette to roasted peppers and olives and toss to coat. Cover and refrigerate. Bring to room temperature before serving. This salad is best made ahead to allow the flavours to blend.

Sesame Broccoli & Red Pepper Salad

• 4 TO 6 SERVINGS •

Broccoli and sweet red pepper are an unbeatable combination for colour, flavour, and nutrition. Research has confirmed what my mother always told me: eat your broccoli; it's good for you. Broccoli delivers many important nutrients, such as vitamin C, beta carotene, vitamin E, folate, fibre, iron, phosphorus, and calcium. Red pepper is also a nutrition powerhouse.

INGREDIENTS

2 Tbsp (30 mL) fresh orange juice

1 Tbsp (15 mL) fresh lemon juice

1 Tbsp (15 mL) unseasoned rice wine vinegar

1 Tbsp (15 mL) liquid honey

1 Tbsp (15 mL) toasted sesame oil

2 tsp (10 mL) low-sodium soy sauce

1 garlic clove, minced

1 large head broccoli, cut in small florets (about 6 cups/1.5 L)

1 sweet red pepper, sliced thinly

2 Tbsp (30 mL) toasted sesame or sunflower seeds (see tip page 8)

1. **FOR THE DRESSING:** whisk together orange juice, lemon juice, rice wine vinegar, honey, sesame oil, soy sauce, and garlic in a small bowl and set aside. If making ahead, cover and refrigerate for up to 4 days.

2. Steam broccoli florets in a medium saucepan until tender-crisp (see tip below). Rinse under running cold water and place on paper towels to dry.

3. Place broccoli florets and sliced red pepper in a large serving bowl and toss with dressing. Sprinkle with toasted sesame seeds. Can be made ahead, then covered and refrigerated for up to 2 days. Serve cold or at room temperature.

TIP Use a collapsible steamer rack in your saucepan to steam the broccoli. Add water to below the level of the rack, bring to a boil, add broccoli, and cover tightly. Steam broccoli until just tender-crisp. This will help it retain its nutrients and bright colour. The sesame dressing is also wonderful served on asparagus or green beans.

Down-East Creamy Potato Salad

This book would not be complete without my sister's potato salad recipe. Potatoes were a staple at our childhood home in Grand Falls, New Brunswick. I have some good and not-so-good memories of early mornings in the potato fields picking potatoes for pocket money as a teenager.

INGREDIENTS

2 lb (1 kg) small white- or red-skinned potatoes

½ cup (125 mL) low-fat yogurt or sour cream
½ cup (125 mL) buttermilk
2 Tbsp (30 mL) fresh lemon juice
2 Tbsp (30 mL) low-fat mayonnaise
2 Tbsp (30 mL) finely chopped fresh flat-leaf parsley
2 Tbsp (30 mL) finely chopped pickles
2 Tbsp (30 mL) finely chopped shallots
2 Tbsp (30 mL) chopped fresh tarragon, mint, or dill
1 tsp (5 mL) Dijon mustard
sea salt and freshly ground pepper

4 hard-boiled eggs, chilled and coarsely chopped (see tip page 8)
1 cup (250 mL) chopped celery
4 to 6 small radishes, cut in half and thinly sliced
2 green onions, thinly sliced

1 Cook potatoes in a large saucepan of boiling, salted water until tender, but still firm, about 15 minutes. Drain potatoes into a colander and let cool for at least 20 minutes. Once cooled, dice potatoes and place them in a large bowl.

2 FOR THE DRESSING: whisk together yogurt, buttermilk, lemon juice, mayonnaise, parsley, pickles, shallots, tarragon, and mustard. Season with salt and pepper to taste.

3 Pour dressing over potatoes and toss. Add chopped eggs, celery, radishes, and green onions and toss gently to combine. Chill until ready to serve.

TIP Choose potatoes that are all about the same size to ensure even cooking. If you prefer, you can substitute an additional ½ cup (125 mL) yogurt or sour cream for the buttermilk in the dressing. Make this salad ahead to give the flavours time to blend; store in the refrigerator and enjoy within 2 days.

Roasted Potato Salad with Peas & Crispy Prosciutto

• 4 TO 6 SERVINGS •

An ideal salad for a barbecue on a hot summer's day. Potatoes are loaded with vitamin C, especially in the skins. They are high in minerals such as potassium, as well as in fibre and complex carbohydrates. You can substitute bacon for the prosciutto and add crumbled feta for a different taste experience.

INGREDIENTS

4   oz (125 g) thinly sliced prosciutto

1½ lb (750 g) small red-skinned
      potatoes, halved
2   Tbsp (30 mL) extra virgin olive oil
sea salt and freshly ground pepper

2   Tbsp (30 mL) champagne vinegar or
      good-quality white wine vinegar
1   Tbsp (15 mL) minced shallot
2   Tbsp (30 mL) extra virgin olive oil

1   cup (250 mL) cooked fresh baby
      peas or thawed frozen peas
2   Tbsp (30 mL) chopped fresh mint or
      tarragon
sea salt and freshly ground pepper

1   Position oven rack in the centre of the oven. Preheat oven to 400°F (200°C).

2   Place prosciutto in a single layer on a baking sheet lined with foil or parchment paper. Roast prosciutto until crisp, about 4 minutes. Set aside to cool and then crumble.

3   Place potatoes on a rimmed baking sheet. Drizzle with olive oil and sprinkle with salt and pepper to taste. Roll potatoes to evenly coat and then spread them in a single layer, cut side down. Roast until tender when pierced with a fork, about 30 minutes.

4   FOR THE VINAIGRETTE: combine vinegar and shallot in a large bowl. Gradually whisk in olive oil until combined.

5   Add warm potatoes to vinaigrette and toss to coat. Add peas, mint, and prosciutto. Toss to combine and adjust seasonings. Serve at room temperature.

Roasted Squash Salad with Maple-Ginger Dressing

This salad is a knockout—great with pork, chicken, or turkey. It makes a wonderful side dish for the holidays, and you can serve it warm or at room temperature. Your kitchen will smell sensational! If making ahead, hold off on adding the pecans until just before serving to maintain their crunch.

INGREDIENTS

2   Tbsp (30 mL) extra virgin olive oil

1   large or 2 small butternut or buttercup squash (about 2 lb/1 kg), peeled and cut into bite-sized cubes

2   red onions, peeled, each cut into 8 wedges

1-inch (2.5 cm) piece of fresh ginger, cut in julienne strips (about ¼ cup/60 mL)

½   tsp (2 mL) sea salt

½   tsp (2 mL) freshly ground pepper

1   Tbsp (15 mL) sherry vinegar or red wine vinegar

1   Tbsp (15 mL) fresh lemon juice

1   Tbsp (15 mL) pure maple syrup

1   tsp (5 mL) minced fresh ginger

2   Tbsp (30 mL) extra virgin olive oil

½   cup (125 mL) coarsely chopped toasted pecans (see tip page 8)

½   cup (125 mL) dried cranberries

sea salt and freshly ground pepper

1   Position a rack in the centre of the oven and preheat to 400°F (200°C).

2   Combine olive oil, squash, onions, ginger, and salt and pepper in a large bowl. Toss well to combine. Spread vegetables out on a large, rimmed baking sheet. Roast for 35 to 40 minutes, or until golden and cooked through, turning vegetables halfway through the cooking time. Remove the roasted vegetables to a serving bowl.

3   FOR THE DRESSING: combine vinegar, lemon juice, maple syrup, and ginger. Gradually whisk in olive oil until well combined.

4   Add dressing to vegetables and toss to coat. Lightly toss in pecans and cranberries, and season with salt and pepper to taste.

TIP You can cut the squash and onions the night before and place them in a large Ziploc bag. Wrap julienne ginger tightly in plastic wrap. The dressing can be covered and refrigerated up to 4 days.

Grain, Pasta, Rice & Bean Salads

Barley Salad with Watercress, Mint, Feta & Black Olives

This is one of my daughter's favourite grain salads. The peppery bite of watercress, the cool taste of mint, and the bold flavour of feta make a great combination. Barley is a good source of fibre, folate, and vitamin E.

INGREDIENTS

3 cups (750 mL) low-sodium chicken stock

1 cup (250 mL) pearl barley

3 Tbsp (45 mL) fresh lemon juice

1 tsp (5 mL) lemon zest

1 garlic clove, minced

2 Tbsp (30 mL) extra virgin olive oil

sea salt and freshly ground pepper

1 bunch watercress, larger stems removed

1 sweet red pepper, diced

1 small English cucumber, diced

½ cup (125 mL) chopped black olives or oil-packed sun-dried tomatoes

½ medium sweet onion, diced

2 Tbsp (30 mL) chopped fresh mint

1 cup (250 mL) diced feta

1 Bring stock to a boil in a medium saucepan. Stir in barley. Reduce heat to medium-low; cover and cook for 25 to 30 minutes, stirring occasionally, until barley is tender but still firm to the bite. Drain any excess liquid. Transfer to a large serving bowl and refrigerate until cool.

2 FOR THE VINAIGRETTE: whisk together lemon juice, lemon zest, garlic, and olive oil in a small bowl. Season with salt and pepper to taste. Set aside.

3 Once barley is cooled, add watercress, red pepper, cucumber, olives, onion, mint, and cheese. Toss with vinaigrette. If making salad ahead, cover and refrigerate up to 3 days. Bring to room temperature before serving.

Wheatberry Salad with Apricots & Pecans

• 4 TO 6 SERVINGS •

Wheatberries are whole kernels of wheat. They have a nutty flavour and are pleasantly chewy. Look for them at health food stores. This is a great make-ahead salad, but hold off on adding the pecans until just before serving to maintain their crunch.

INGREDIENTS

6 cups (1.5 L) water
1 cup (250 mL) wheatberries
½ tsp (2 mL) sea salt

1 tsp (5 mL) Dijon mustard
1 Tbsp (15 mL) finely chopped shallot
   or green onion
1 tsp (5 mL) orange zest
½ cup (125 mL) fresh orange juice
2 Tbsp (30 mL) chopped fresh flat-leaf
   parsley, cilantro, or mint
1 Tbsp (15 mL) balsamic vinegar
1 Tbsp (15 mL) extra virgin olive oil
sea salt and freshly ground pepper

⅓ cup (80 mL) chopped dried apricots
⅓ cup (80 mL) chopped toasted pecans
   (see tip page 8)

1 Bring water to a boil in a large saucepan. Add wheatberries and salt; cook uncovered over low heat for approximately 45 minutes, or until soft but still firm to the bite. Drain well using a colander, then transfer to a medium bowl. Let cool to room temperature.

2 FOR THE VINAIGRETTE: combine mustard, shallot, orange zest, orange juice, parsley, and balsamic vinegar in a small bowl. Whisk in olive oil until well combined. Season with salt and pepper to taste and set aside. If making ahead, cover and refrigerate up to 4 days.

3 Add vinaigrette, apricots, and pecans to the wheatberries. Toss to combine. If making ahead, cover and refrigerate up to 3 days.

One of the very nicest things about life is the way we must regularly stop whatever it is we are doing and devote our attention to eating. —LUCIANO PAVAROTTI

Asian-Style Brown Rice Salad

Brown rice has a wonderful chewy texture and is rich in B vitamins, protein, magnesium, and fibre. Combined with edamame and a ginger-sesame dressing, it makes a flavourful and nutritious salad. You can also add black beans for a delicious vegetarian main dish. If you're making the salad ahead, add the almonds just before serving to maintain their crunch.

INGREDIENTS

¾ cup (185 mL) brown rice

2 cups (500 mL) water

¼ tsp (1 mL) sea salt

1 large garlic clove, minced

1 tsp (5 mL) minced fresh ginger

2 Tbsp (30 mL) fresh lemon juice

1 Tbsp (15 mL) low-sodium soy sauce

1 Tbsp (15 mL) liquid honey

1 Tbsp (15 mL) toasted sesame oil

pinch of red chili flakes

1 cup (250 mL) shelled, cooked edamame (see tip below) or frozen thawed peas

1 cup (250 mL) finely diced carrots

2 green onions, finely chopped

½ cup (125 mL) toasted slivered almonds (see tip page 8)

3 Tbsp (45 mL) chopped fresh cilantro or flat-leaf parsley

1 Combine rice, water, and salt in a medium saucepan and bring to a boil over high heat. Reduce heat to low, cover, and simmer for 30 minutes. Remove from heat and let stand, covered, for 10 minutes (rice will be tender but still firm to the bite). Fluff rice with a fork and transfer to a large bowl to cool.

2 FOR THE DRESSING: whisk together garlic, ginger, lemon juice, soy sauce, honey, sesame oil, and chili flakes in a small bowl. Set aside. If making ahead, cover and refrigerate for up to 4 days.

3 Add dressing, edamame, carrots, green onions, almonds, and cilantro to the rice. The salad can be made earlier in the day, then covered and refrigerated. Bring to room temperature before serving.

TIP Edamame are young green soybeans. You can find them shelled in the freezer case in most grocery stores. Steam the frozen beans for 3 minutes, and they are ready to go.

Fiesta Rice Salad

Spicy dressing, black beans, corn, and peppers add a Mexican touch to this high-fibre, low-fat, nutrient-packed rice salad. Perfect for picnics or to take along to a potluck.

INGREDIENTS

1   tsp (5 mL) grapeseed or safflower oil
1   cup (250 mL) long-grain white rice
2   cups (500 mL) boiling water

1   jalapeño pepper, seeded
    and chopped
2   garlic cloves, minced
1   tsp (5 mL) chili powder
¼   cup (60 mL) fresh lime juice
2   Tbsp (30 mL) grapeseed or
    safflower oil
sea salt and freshly ground pepper

19 oz (540 mL) black beans, drained
    and rinsed
12 oz (355 mL) can corn, drained
    and rinsed
1   cup (250 mL) frozen peas, thawed
1   sweet orange or red pepper, diced
4   green onions, finely sliced
¼   cup (60 mL) chopped fresh flat-leaf
    parsley or cilantro

1   Heat oil over medium heat in a saucepan. Add rice and stir to coat. Add boiling water. Cover and simmer for 20 minutes, or until water is absorbed and rice is tender. Transfer to a large bowl to cool.

2   FOR THE DRESSING: combine jalapeño, garlic, chili powder, and lime juice in a small bowl. Gradually whisk in oil until well combined, and season with salt and pepper to taste. Set aside. If making ahead, cover and refrigerate for up to 4 days.

3   Add beans, corn, peas, orange pepper, green onions, parsley, and dressing to rice and toss to coat. If making ahead, cover and refrigerate. Bring to room temperature before serving.

Wild Rice Salad with Pine Nuts & Mint

• 4 SERVINGS •

Wild rice is not really rice at all but an aquatic grain harvested from a long-stemmed annual plant that grows primarily in the shallow waters of northern Ontario, Manitoba, and Minnesota. This colourful, healthy salad has a distinctive flavour and wonderful texture. If you're making it ahead, add the pine nuts just before serving to maintain their crunch.

INGREDIENTS

½ cup (125 mL) wild rice
4 cups (1 L) water
½ cup (125 mL) long-grain white rice

2 tsp (10 mL) Dijon mustard
1 garlic clove, minced
1 tsp (5 mL) lemon zest
2 Tbsp (30 mL) fresh lemon juice
2 tsp (10 mL) liquid honey
2 Tbsp (30 mL) extra virgin olive oil
sea salt and freshly ground pepper

½ cup (125 mL) finely diced carrot
½ cup (125 mL) finely diced celery
¼ cup (60 mL) finely diced red onion
¼ cup (60 mL) toasted pine nuts or chopped toasted pecans (see tip page 8)
¼ cup (60 mL) chopped fresh mint
2 Tbsp (30 mL) chopped fresh flat-leaf parsley

1 Rinse wild rice in a colander under cold water. Bring water to a boil in a large saucepan. Stir in wild rice, cover, and let cook undisturbed for 15 minutes. Stir in white rice and cook, covered, for another 20 minutes. Remove from heat and let sit, covered, for another 5 minutes to let rice absorb the water. Remove the lid, stir to fluff rice, and let cool to room temperature.

2 FOR THE VINAIGRETTE: combine mustard, garlic, lemon zest, lemon juice, and honey in a small bowl. Gradually whisk in olive oil until well combined, and season with salt and pepper to taste. Set aside.

3 Combine rice, carrot, celery, onion, pine nuts, mint, and parsley in a large bowl. Toss with vinaigrette. If making ahead, cover and refrigerate for up to 3 days.

Quinoa Salad with Mango, Peanuts & Currants

Quinoa, pronounced keen-wah, *is very nutritious. It's a complete protein, which is especially important to vegetarians. It's also high in calcium and iron. You can find quinoa in well-stocked supermarkets or in health food stores. Assembling this salad early in the day, or even the day before, will give the ingredients a chance to meld and develop more flavour.*

INGREDIENTS

2 cups (500 mL) water
1 cup (250 mL) quinoa
¼ tsp (1 mL) sea salt

1 garlic clove, minced
1 Tbsp (15 mL) fresh lemon juice
1 Tbsp (15 mL) toasted sesame oil
1 tsp (5 mL) liquid honey
sea salt and freshly ground pepper

1 ripe mango, cut into small cubes (see tip page 5)
1 jalapeño pepper, seeded and finely chopped
½ cup (125 mL) finely chopped sweet red pepper
¼ cup (60 mL) finely chopped red onion
¼ cup (60 mL) dried currants
2 Tbsp (30 mL) chopped fresh flat-leaf parsley
½ cup (125 mL) chopped peanuts

1 Bring water to a boil in a large saucepan. Add quinoa and salt; cook over medium heat, stirring occasionally, until tender but still firm to the bite, about 12 minutes. Drain well. Transfer to a medium bowl and let cool to room temperature.

2 FOR THE VINAIGRETTE: whisk together garlic, lemon juice, sesame oil, and honey in a small bowl until well combined. Season with salt and pepper. Set aside.

3 Add mango, jalapeño, red pepper, red onion, currants, parsley, and vinaigrette to quinoa and toss to combine. Add peanuts just before serving. If making ahead, cover and refrigerate. Bring to room temperature before serving.

Lemony Herbed Quinoa Salad

This is a refreshing and tasty salad. You can make it into a completely balanced meal by topping it with grilled chicken, steak, or seafood. The salad will improve in flavour if made ahead of time.

INGREDIENTS

2 cups (500 mL) water
1 cup (250 mL) quinoa
¼ tsp (1 mL) sea salt

1 tsp (5 mL) Dijon mustard
¼ cup (60 mL) fresh lemon juice
¼ cup (60 mL) finely chopped fresh mint
¼ cup (60 mL) finely chopped fresh cilantro
2 Tbsp (30 mL) grapeseed or safflower oil
sea salt and freshly ground pepper

½ cucumber, peeled and diced
½ sweet red pepper, diced
1 stalk celery, diced
½ cup (125 mL) diced red onion

1   Bring water to a boil in a large saucepan. Add quinoa and salt; simmer over medium heat, stirring occasionally, until tender but still firm to the bite, about 12 minutes. Drain well, transfer to a medium-sized bowl, and let cool to room temperature.

2   FOR THE VINAIGRETTE: combine mustard, lemon juice, mint, and cilantro in a small bowl. Gradually whisk in oil until well combined, and season with salt and pepper to taste. Set aside. If making ahead, cover and refrigerate for up to 4 days.

3   Add cucumber, red pepper, celery, red onion, and vinaigrette to quinoa and toss to combine. If making ahead, cover and refrigerate up to 2 days. Bring to room temperature before serving.

Quinoa Salad with Cranberries & Pistachio Nuts

Quinoa was considered sacred by the Incas, and it's no wonder: it is packed with protein and also contains calcium and iron. If you're making this salad ahead, add the pistachio nuts just before serving to maintain their crunch.

INGREDIENTS

2 cups (500 mL) water
1 cup (250 mL) quinoa
¼ tsp (1 mL) sea salt

2 Tbsp (30 mL) fresh orange juice
1 tsp (5 mL) orange zest
2 Tbsp (30 mL) fresh lemon juice
1 Tbsp (15 mL) liquid honey
¼ tsp (1 mL) hot pepper sauce
2 Tbsp (30 mL) extra virgin olive oil
sea salt and freshly ground pepper

2 green onions, finely chopped
½ cup (125 mL) coarsely chopped
   dried cranberries
2 Tbsp (30 mL) chopped fresh mint or
   flat-leaf parsley
½ cup (125 mL) chopped toasted
   pistachio nuts (see tip page 8)

1 Bring water to a boil in a large saucepan. Add quinoa and salt; cook over medium heat, stirring occasionally, until tender but still firm to the bite, about 12 minutes. Drain well. Transfer to a medium bowl and let cool to room temperature.

2 FOR THE DRESSING: whisk together orange juice and zest, lemon juice, honey, and hot pepper sauce in a small bowl. Gradually whisk in olive oil until well combined, and season with salt and pepper to taste. Set aside.

3 Add green onions, cranberries, mint, and dressing to quinoa and toss to combine. Just before serving, add pistachio nuts. If making ahead, cover and refrigerate for up to 2 days.

An inordinate passion for pleasure is the secret of remaining young. —OSCAR WILDE

Curried Couscous & Corn Salad

Here is a great way to use versatile, healthy couscous. This is a dish that gets even better after it sits for a few hours to give the flavours time to blend.

INGREDIENTS

1¼ cups (310 mL) water

1 cup (250 mL) couscous

1 tsp (5 mL) Indian curry paste or powder

1 tsp (5 mL) Dijon mustard

1 Tbsp (15 mL) fresh lemon juice

1 Tbsp (15 mL) sherry vinegar or red wine vinegar

2 Tbsp (30 mL) grapeseed or safflower oil

sea salt and freshly ground pepper

1 Tbsp (15 mL) grapeseed oil

1 cup (250 mL) diced sweet onion

2 large garlic cloves, minced

1 jalapeño pepper, seeded and finely chopped

½ sweet red pepper, finely chopped

3 cups (750 mL) corn kernels, fresh, frozen, or canned

¼ cup (60 mL) chopped fresh cilantro or flat-leaf parsley

1 Bring water to a boil in a medium saucepan. Stir in couscous and remove from heat. Cover and let stand for 10 minutes. Fluff couscous with a fork, transfer to a large bowl, and set aside to cool.

2 FOR THE DRESSING: combine curry paste, mustard, lemon juice, and vinegar in a medium bowl. Gradually whisk in oil until well combined. Season with salt and pepper to taste and set aside.

3 Heat oil in a large skillet over medium heat. Add onion, garlic, jalapeño, and red pepper and sauté for 4 minutes, or until onion has softened. Stir in corn and cook another 2 minutes.

4 Stir corn mixture into couscous. Add dressing and cilantro. Toss to combine. Serve at room temperature.

101

Moroccan Couscous Salad

Couscous comes alive in a salad with fragrant spices, lemon, crunchy red pepper, almonds, and a hint of sweetness from the currants. Make this salad early in the day, or the day before, to give the flavours time to blend.

INGREDIENTS

1¼ cups (310 mL) low-sodium chicken
    stock or water
1 Tbsp (15 mL) extra virgin olive oil
½ tsp (2 mL) ground cumin
¼ tsp (1 mL) ground cinnamon
1 cup (250 mL) couscous

1 garlic clove, minced
1 tsp (5 mL) lemon zest
3 Tbsp (45 mL) fresh lemon juice
2 Tbsp (30 mL) extra virgin olive oil
sea salt and freshly ground pepper

½ cup (125 mL) diced sweet
    red pepper
⅓ cup (80 mL) finely chopped
    green onions
⅓ cup (80 mL) dried currants or
    finely chopped dried apricots
½ cup (125 mL) chopped fresh cilantro,
    flat-leaf parsley, or mint
¼ cup (60 mL) toasted slivered almonds
    or pine nuts (see tip page 8)

1 Bring chicken stock, olive oil, cumin, and cinnamon to a boil in a medium saucepan. Stir in couscous and remove from heat. Cover and let stand for 10 minutes. Fluff couscous with a fork, transfer to a large bowl, and let cool to room temperature.

2 FOR THE VINAIGRETTE: combine garlic, lemon zest, and lemon juice in a small bowl. Gradually whisk in olive oil until well combined and season with salt and pepper to taste. Set aside. If making ahead, cover and refrigerate for up to 4 days.

3 Combine red pepper, green onions, currants, cilantro, and almonds with couscous and toss with vinaigrette. If making ahead, cover and refrigerate for up to 3 days. This salad is best served at room temperature.

Israeli Couscous Salad with Sun-Dried Tomatoes & Pine Nuts

Israeli couscous, also called pearl couscous, is larger than the North African variety and has a chewy texture. You can substitute orzo (rice-shaped pasta). Using the oil from the sun-dried tomatoes infuses this salad with flavour. A perfect side dish to meat, poultry, or fish.

INGREDIENTS

1 Tbsp (15 mL) extra virgin olive oil

1 large garlic clove, minced

2 cups (500 mL) Israeli couscous

3 cups (750 mL) low-sodium chicken or vegetable stock

3 Tbsp (45 mL) fresh lemon juice

1 tsp (5 mL) lemon zest

6 oil-packed sun-dried tomato halves, finely chopped

2 Tbsp (30 mL) oil from the sun-dried tomatoes

freshly ground pepper

½ cup (125 mL) chopped fresh mint

½ cup (125 mL) chopped fresh basil

⅓ cup (80 mL) toasted pine nuts or slivered almonds (see tip page 8)

1 Heat olive oil in a saucepan over medium-low heat. Add garlic and couscous. Cook, stirring, for about 4 minutes, until the couscous is just slightly toasted and golden. Add stock and bring to a boil. Reduce the heat and simmer, covered, until couscous is tender but still firm to the bite, about 8 minutes. Drain couscous using a colander.

2 In a medium bowl, toss cooked couscous with lemon juice and zest, sun-dried tomatoes, and oil from the tomatoes. Season with pepper and let cool to room temperature. If making ahead, cover and refrigerate up to 2 days.

3 Just before serving, add mint, basil, and pine nuts.

TIP If you choose to use orzo, you only need 1½ cups (375 mL) since orzo absorbs more liquid than Israeli couscous.

Pasta & Chickpea Salad with Roasted Red Pepper Dressing

Roasting red peppers takes a little time, but it is well worth the effort. Double up on the dressing—it keeps for up to a week in the refrigerator, and it is also wonderful tossed with romaine lettuce, chicken, and Parmesan cheese.

INGREDIENTS

1 cup (250 mL) chopped roasted sweet red peppers (about 2 large peppers; see tip page 6)

1 garlic clove, chopped

2 Tbsp (30 mL) extra virgin olive oil

1 Tbsp (15 mL) balsamic vinegar

1 tsp (5 mL) liquid honey

sea salt and freshly ground pepper

2 cups (500 mL) uncooked tricolour fusilli, rotini, or bow-tie pasta

1 cup (250 mL) chickpeas, drained and rinsed

½ English cucumber, diced

½ cup (125 mL) diced feta or coarsely grated fresh Parmesan cheese

¼ cup (60 mL) chopped kalamata olives or chopped oil-packed sun-dried tomatoes

¼ cup (60 mL) chopped fresh basil

1 FOR THE DRESSING: place roasted red peppers, garlic, oil, vinegar, and honey in a food processor or blender. Blend just until smooth, and season with salt and pepper to taste. Set aside. (If you don't have a blender, chop peppers finely and combine with minced garlic, vinegar, and honey. Whisk in oil until well combined and season with salt and pepper.) If making ahead, cover and refrigerate for up to 4 days.

2 Bring a large saucepan of salted water to a boil. Add pasta and cook until al dente. Drain pasta and rinse under cold running water. Place in a large bowl and toss with the dressing.

3 Add chickpeas, cucumber, feta, olives, and basil to the pasta. Toss to coat. If making ahead, cover and refrigerate up to 2 days. Best served at room temperature.

Antipasto Pasta Salad

This appetizing pasta salad looks fantastic on a buffet table and can easily be doubled if you are feeding a crowd. Capocollo is a delicious Italian-style cured ham; look for it sliced in the deli section of your supermarket. If you're making the salad ahead, add the arugula just before serving.

INGREDIENTS

3 cups (750 mL) uncooked fusilli or rotini pasta

1 tsp (5 mL) Dijon mustard
2 Tbsp (30 mL) finely chopped shallots
1 garlic clove, minced
3 Tbsp (45 mL) sherry vinegar or red wine vinegar
3 Tbsp (45 mL) extra virgin olive oil
sea salt and freshly ground pepper

2 roasted sweet red peppers, cut into thin strips (see tip page 6)
2 cups (500 mL) baby arugula
1½ cups (375 mL) diced bocconcini (fresh mozzarella cheese balls)
1 cup (250 mL) diced *capocollo* or other Italian-style cured ham
½ cup (125 mL) brine-cured or kalamata olives, pitted and chopped

1 Bring a large saucepan of salted water to a boil. Add pasta and cook until al dente. Drain pasta and cool immediately under cold running water. Place in a large serving bowl.

2 FOR THE VINAIGRETTE: combine mustard, shallots, garlic, and vinegar in a small bowl. Gradually whisk in olive oil until well combined, and season with salt and pepper to taste.

3 Add vinaigrette, red pepper strips, arugula, bocconcini, ham, and olives to pasta and toss gently to coat. If making ahead, cover and refrigerate up to 3 days. This salad is best served at room temperature.

We are not permitted to choose the frame of our destiny. But what we put into it is ours. —DAG HAMMARSKJOLD

Niçoise Pasta Salad

A wonderful summer salad your family and friends will enjoy.
Pasta is a nutritious food; it contains almost no fat, cholesterol,
or sodium and is an excellent source of energy-giving carbohydrates.
Tuna provides you with omega-3 essential fatty acids.

INGREDIENTS

1   small bunch asparagus, cut in 1-inch
    (2.5 cm) pieces, about 2 cups (500 mL),
    or substitute frozen peas, thawed
3   cups (750 mL) uncooked fusilli, rotini,
    or bow-tie pasta

1   tsp (5 mL) Dijon mustard
1   garlic clove, minced
3   Tbsp (45 mL) fresh lemon juice
1   Tbsp (15 mL) balsamic vinegar
2   Tbsp (30 mL) extra virgin olive oil
sea salt and freshly ground pepper

1   cup (250 mL) quartered grape or
    cherry tomatoes
6   oz (170 g) can solid white tuna packed in oil,
    drained and broken in chunks
4   anchovy fillets, minced, OR 2 Tbsp (30 mL)
    capers
¼   cup (60 mL) diced red onion
¼   cup (60 mL) niçoise olives or pitted, sliced
    kalamata olives
¼   cup (60 mL) chopped fresh flat-leaf parsley

1 In a large saucepan of boiling, salted water, cook asparagus for 2 to 3 minutes, or until tender-crisp. Remove asparagus with a slotted spoon and rinse under cold water. Pat dry and set aside. Add pasta to boiling water and cook until al dente. Drain and rinse under cold water. Transfer to a large bowl.

2 FOR THE VINAIGRETTE: combine mustard, garlic, lemon juice, and vinegar in a small bowl. Whisk in oil until well combined, and season with salt and pepper to taste. Set aside.

3 Add tomatoes, tuna, anchovies, red onion, olives, parsley, and asparagus to the pasta. Toss with vinaigrette. Serve at room temperature. This salad is best served the day it is made.

Pasta & Chicken Salad with Basil Vinaigrette

• 4 TO 6 SERVINGS •

This is the perfect pasta salad to take along to a potluck meal. It is a crowd pleaser—even your kids will enjoy it! You can substitute shrimp or tuna for the chicken.

INGREDIENTS

3 cups (750 mL) uncooked gemelli, fusilli, or bow-tie pasta

½ cup (125 mL) coarsely chopped fresh basil

2 Tbsp (30 mL) balsamic vinegar

2 Tbsp (30 mL) fresh lemon juice

1 tsp (5 mL) Dijon mustard

¼ cup (60 mL) extra virgin olive oil

2 Tbsp (30 mL) finely chopped shallots or red onion

sea salt and freshly ground pepper

1½ cups (375 mL) chopped or shredded cooked chicken

1 cup (250 mL) cherry or grape tomatoes, halved

1 small zucchini, quartered lengthwise and cut crosswise into thin slices

½ cup (125 mL) coarsely grated fresh Parmesan cheese

1 Bring a large saucepan of salted water to a boil. Add pasta and cook until al dente. Drain and rinse under cold running water. Transfer to a large bowl.

2 FOR THE VINAIGRETTE: in a food processor, purée basil with vinegar, lemon juice, and mustard. Blend in olive oil. (If you don't have a food processor, chop basil finely and pound to a paste with a little salt before mixing with the rest of the ingredients.) Pour the dressing in a small bowl, add shallots, and season with salt and pepper to taste. Set aside. If making ahead, cover and refrigerate up to 4 days.

3 Add chicken, tomatoes, zucchini, Parmesan cheese, and vinaigrette to the pasta. Toss to combine. If making ahead, cover and refrigerate up to 2 days. Best served at room temperature.

Italian Bean & Tuna Salad

This tasty, colourful salad is satisfying and packed with protein and vitamins. Beans are a high-quality source of protein and a good source of heart-healthy dietary fibre, while the tuna supplies omega-3 essential fatty acids. Make this salad early in the day to let the beans and tuna marinate in the dressing.

INGREDIENTS

2 garlic cloves, minced

1 tsp (5 mL) lemon zest

¼ cup (60 mL) fresh lemon juice

3 Tbsp (45 mL) extra virgin olive oil

sea salt and freshly ground pepper

two 19 oz (540 mL) cans cannellini
   (white kidney) beans, drained
   and rinsed

½ red onion, thinly sliced

1 cup (250 mL) grape or cherry
   tomatoes, halved

⅓ cup (80 mL) capers, drained
   and rinsed

½ cup (125 mL) chopped fresh flat-leaf
   parsley or cilantro

4 cups (1 L) torn heart of romaine
   lettuce

two 6 oz (170 g) cans solid white tuna,
   drained, broken into bite-sized pieces

1 FOR THE VINAIGRETTE: combine garlic, lemon zest, and lemon juice in a small bowl. Gradually whisk in oil until well combined. Season with salt and pepper to taste and set aside. If making ahead, cover and refrigerate for up to 4 days.

2 Combine beans, onion, tomatoes, capers, and parsley in a large bowl. Gently toss with half the vinaigrette. If making ahead, cover and refrigerate until ready to serve.

3 Just before serving, scatter lettuce on a large serving platter. Top with bean salad and arrange tuna on top. Drizzle remaining vinaigrette over tuna.

Bean Medley Salad

This simple, satisfying salad has a delicious combination of flavours. An important source of protein and fibre, beans also provide folic acid, iron, and potassium. They are low in fat and contain no cholesterol.

INGREDIENTS

1 cup (250 mL) green beans, trimmed and cut into thirds

1 cup (250 mL) yellow (wax) beans, trimmed and cut into thirds

19 oz (540 mL) can mixed beans, drained and rinsed

2 green onions, finely chopped

6 oil-packed sun-dried tomato halves, finely chopped (reserve oil for dressing)

¼ cup (60 mL) pitted, chopped kalamata olives

2 garlic cloves, minced

2 Tbsp (30 mL) chopped fresh basil or parsley

3 Tbsp (45 mL) fresh lemon juice

2 Tbsp (30 mL) oil from the sun-dried tomatoes

sea salt and freshly ground pepper

1 Cook green and yellow beans in a large saucepan of boiling water just until tender-crisp, about 4 minutes. Drain and refresh under cold water. Pat dry with paper towels and place in a large bowl.

2 Add mixed beans, green onions, sun-dried tomatoes, and olives. Set aside.

3 FOR THE VINAIGRETTE: combine garlic, basil, and lemon juice in a small bowl. Whisk in sun-dried tomato oil until well combined, and season with salt and pepper to taste.

4 Add vinaigrette to salad and refrigerate, covered, until ready to serve. Can be made up to 2 days ahead.

Asian-Style Bean Salad

This Asian-inspired salad is bursting with flavour and loaded with healthy ingredients. For a lovely presentation, serve this salad in leaves of Boston lettuce. To complete your meal, top the salad with chunks of grilled tuna, salmon, or chicken.

INGREDIENTS

1   large garlic clove, minced
½   tsp (2 mL) grated fresh ginger
3   Tbsp (45 mL) fresh lime juice
1   tsp (5 mL) low-sodium soy sauce
2   Tbsp (30 mL) grapeseed oil
1   Tbsp (15 mL) toasted sesame oil
freshly ground pepper

4   cups (1 L) yellow beans, sliced
    in 1-inch (2.5 cm) lengths
3   cups (750 mL) frozen shelled
    edamame

1   sweet red pepper, diced
2   green onions, finely chopped
2   Tbsp (30 mL) chopped fresh cilantro
    or flat-leaf parsley

1   FOR THE DRESSING: whisk together garlic, ginger, lime juice, soy sauce, grapeseed oil, and sesame oil in a small bowl. Season with pepper to taste and set aside.

2   Cook beans and edamame in a large saucepan of boiling water just until tender-crisp, about 3 minutes. Drain and refresh under cold water. Pat dry with paper towels, place in a large bowl, and refrigerate for 15 minutes.

3   Add red pepper, green onions, and cilantro to the beans and toss with dressing to coat. The flavour of this salad will improve if you make it a few hours before serving.

French Lentil Salad with Bacon

The sweetness of maple syrup and robust flavour of crisp bacon make this salad irresistible and ideal to serve with roasted meats or poultry. French lentils, also called du Puy lentils, can be found in well-stocked supermarkets or health food stores. They have a wonderful nutty taste and keep their shape well, making them ideal to use in salads. Lentils are rich in iron and vitamin C.

INGREDIENTS

1   cup (250 mL) French (du Puy) lentils
4   cups (1 L) water
¼   tsp (1 mL) sea salt

6   slices bacon, coarsely chopped

2   carrots, shredded
1   sweet red or yellow pepper, finely diced
⅓   cup (80 mL) finely chopped red onion

⅓   cup (80 mL) finely chopped fresh
    flat-leaf parsley

1   tsp (5 mL) Dijon mustard
3   Tbsp (45 mL) balsamic vinegar
2   Tbsp (30 mL) fresh lemon juice
2   Tbsp (30 mL) pure maple syrup
¼   cup (60 mL) extra virgin olive oil
sea salt and freshly ground pepper

1   Rinse lentils well. In a large saucepan combine water, lentils, and salt. Bring to a boil, reduce heat, and simmer for 20 to 25 minutes, or until lentils are tender. Be careful not to overcook the lentils; check them regularly after 15 minutes of cooking. Drain lentils using a colander and set aside to cool.

2   Cook bacon in a large, heavy skillet over medium heat until brown and crisp. Place on paper towels to cool.

3   Combine lentils with carrots, red pepper, onion, parsley, and bacon in a large serving bowl. Set aside.

4   FOR THE VINAIGRETTE: combine mustard, vinegar, lemon juice, and maple syrup in a small bowl. Gradually whisk in olive oil until well combined, and season with salt and pepper to taste.

5   Toss salad with vinaigrette. If making ahead, cover and refrigerate up to 3 days.

Meat & Chicken Salads

Beef Taco Salad
with Salsa Dressing

My son-in-law, who loves to cook, inspired this wonderful dish—one of our favourite salads to have in the summer. The salsa dressing can be made with mild, medium, or hot salsa.

INGREDIENTS

¾ cup (185 mL) low-fat sour cream

¾ cup (185 mL) salsa

3 Tbsp (45 mL) fresh lime juice

2 Tbsp (30 mL) low-fat mayonnaise

1 Tbsp (15 mL) grapeseed or safflower oil

1 medium onion, chopped

2 garlic cloves, minced

2 tsp (10 mL) Cajun spice

½ tsp (2 mL) sea salt

½ tsp (2 mL) freshly ground pepper

1 lb (500 g) extra-lean ground beef

14 oz (398 mL) can kidney beans, drained and rinsed

1 cup (250 mL) seeded, diced tomatoes

8 cups (2 L) shredded romaine or iceberg lettuce

¼ cup (60 mL) chopped fresh cilantro

1 cup (250 mL) shredded sharp cheddar cheese

1 large ripe avocado, diced (see tip page 5; prepare just before serving)

2 green onions, finely chopped

baked tortilla chips

1 **FOR THE DRESSING:** combine sour cream, salsa, lime juice, and mayonnaise in a small bowl. Set aside, or if making ahead, cover and refrigerate up to 2 days.

2 Heat oil in a large non-stick skillet over medium-high heat. Add onion, garlic, Cajun spice, and salt and pepper. Sauté until softened, about 3 minutes. Add beef and brown, breaking it up with the back of a wooden spoon, until cooked through, about 5 minutes. Drain and place in a large bowl. Add beans, tomatoes, and ¼ cup (60 mL) of the salsa dressing. Combine and set aside.

3 Place lettuce and cilantro in a large bowl and toss with enough salsa dressing to coat (you may not need it all). Divide salad among 6 plates. Top each with beef mixture, cheese, avocado, and green onions. Serve with baked tortilla chips on the side, or scatter coarsely crumbled tortilla chips on top of salads. Serve immediately.

Grilled Sirloin Steak Salad with Sesame-Ginger Dressing

This salad always brings on a big smile from my boys (husband, son, and son-in-law), who love steak. I like to find ways to combine steak with crisp vegetables, greens, and a wonderful tangy dressing to create a main-course salad. This delicious salad could become a favourite with your family, too!

INGREDIENTS

1 garlic clove, minced

2 tsp (10 mL) grated fresh ginger

1 Tbsp (15 mL) low-sodium soy sauce

1 Tbsp (15 mL) balsamic vinegar

2 tsp (10 mL) toasted sesame oil

2 tsp (10 mL) brown sugar

1 lb (500 g) top sirloin steak, 1 inch (2.5 cm) thick

2 Tbsp (30 mL) teriyaki sauce

6 cups (1.5 L) mixed baby greens

1 sweet red pepper, thinly sliced

½ English cucumber, halved lengthwise and thinly sliced

3 green onions, thinly sliced

1 **FOR THE DRESSING:** whisk together garlic, ginger, soy sauce, vinegar, sesame oil, and brown sugar in a small bowl. Set aside. If making ahead, cover and refrigerate up to 4 days.

2 Place steak on a large plate and drizzle with teriyaki sauce on both sides. Let sit at room temperature for 20 minutes.

3 Coat a barbecue grate, indoor grill, or grill pan with cooking spray. Grill steak until medium-rare, about 5 minutes per side, or until cooked to your preference. Let rest for 5 minutes, then slice against the grain.

4 Combine baby greens, red pepper, cucumber, and green onions in a large bowl. Toss with dressing to coat and arrange salad on 4 plates. Top with steak slices.

TIP You can add or substitute other vegetables, such as snow peas or snap peas, pea shoots, celery, blanched green beans, broccoli, or asparagus.

Grilled Steak Salad with Tomatoes & Gorgonzola

• 4 MAIN-COURSE SERVINGS •

This is one of our family favourites! I sometimes grill the steak on the stovetop in a grill pan, but when I use the barbecue, I like to grill portobello mushrooms and asparagus along with the steak to add to this delicious salad.

INGREDIENTS

1 tsp (5 mL) Dijon mustard

1 garlic clove, minced

2 Tbsp (30 mL) balsamic vinegar

1 Tbsp (15 mL) liquid honey

1 tsp (5 mL) Worcestershire sauce

¼ cup (60 mL) extra virgin olive oil

1½ lb (750 g) steak, such as New York strip, rib-eye, or top sirloin, 1 inch (2.5 cm) thick

1 Tbsp (15 mL) Worcestershire sauce

6 cups (1.5 L) torn heart of romaine lettuce

2 cups (500 mL) cherry or grape tomatoes, halved

½ cup (125 mL) thinly sliced red onion

½ cup (125 mL) crumbled gorgonzola or blue cheese, or more to taste

1 FOR THE DRESSING: combine mustard, garlic, vinegar, honey, and Worcestershire sauce in a small bowl. Gradually whisk in oil until well combined. Set aside. If making ahead, cover and refrigerate up to 4 days.

2 Place steak on a large plate and drizzle with Worcestershire sauce on both sides. Let sit at room temperature for 20 to 30 minutes.

3 Coat barbecue grate or grill pan with cooking spray. Preheat barbecue, indoor grill, or grill pan to medium-high. Grill steak until medium-rare, about 5 minutes per side, or until done to your preference. Let rest for 5 minutes, then slice against the grain.

4 Just before serving, combine lettuce, tomatoes, and red onion in a large bowl. Toss with just enough dressing to coat (you may not need it all). Arrange salad on a large platter or divide among 4 individual plates. Sprinkle with cheese and top with steak slices.

Mango Chicken Salad with Poppy Seed Vinaigrette

• 4 TO 6 MAIN-COURSE SERVINGS •

Deli-roasted chickens are wonderful on hot days when you don't want to turn on the stove or even light the barbecue. This healthy, nourishing salad offers an exciting mix of flavours, textures, and colours.

INGREDIENTS

1   tsp (5 mL) Dijon mustard

1   tsp (5 mL) orange zest

2   Tbsp (30 mL) fresh orange juice

2   Tbsp (30 mL) white wine vinegar or apple cider vinegar

2   tsp (10 mL) poppy seeds

⅓   cup (80 mL) grapeseed or safflower oil

sea salt and freshly ground pepper

3   cups (750 mL) bite-sized chunks cooked chicken (about 1 small deli-roasted chicken, skinned)

1   large, ripe mango, diced (see tip page 5)

6   cups (1.5 L) torn Boston lettuce or baby romaine

1   red or yellow pepper, cut into small cubes

⅓   cup (80 mL) thinly sliced red onion

½   cup (125 mL) diced feta, or more to taste

½   cup (125 mL) chopped toasted pecans (see tip page 8)

1 **FOR THE VINAIGRETTE:** combine mustard, orange zest, orange juice, vinegar, and poppy seeds. Gradually whisk in grapeseed oil until well combined, and season with salt and pepper to taste. Set aside. If making ahead, cover and refrigerate for up to 4 days.

2 Just before serving, combine chicken, mango, lettuce, yellow pepper, red onion, feta, and pecans in a large serving bowl. Toss with vinaigrette.

TIP You can prepare all ingredients earlier in the day and store them separately in airtight containers or Ziploc bags.

Grilled Chicken & Peach Salad with Creamy Curry Dressing

• 4 MAIN-COURSE SERVINGS •

This is a fresh and exciting salad! Nothing is more delicious than juicy peaches when they are in season. If peaches are not available, you can substitute nectarines, pineapple, or mango.

INGREDIENTS

½ cup (125 mL) low-fat yogurt or sour cream

3 Tbsp (45 mL) fresh lemon juice

2 Tbsp (30 mL) grapeseed or safflower oil

1 Tbsp (15 mL) finely chopped shallot

2 tsp (10 mL) liquid honey

1 tsp (5 mL) minced fresh ginger

1 tsp (5 mL) curry paste or powder

sea salt and freshly ground pepper

2 large ripe peaches

6 cups (1.5 L) mixed baby greens

1 bunch watercress, larger stems removed

1 sweet orange or red pepper, thinly sliced

½ cup (125 mL) thinly sliced red onion

4 grilled or roasted chicken breasts, cut into strips

½ cup (125 mL) coarsely chopped cashews

¼ cup (60 mL) chopped fresh cilantro or mint

1 **FOR THE DRESSING:** whisk together yogurt, lemon juice, grapeseed oil, shallot, honey, ginger, and curry paste in a small bowl. Season with salt and pepper to taste and set aside. If making ahead, cover and refrigerate up to 2 days.

2 Fill a medium saucepan halfway with water and bring to a boil. Drop in peaches for 40 seconds, then remove and rinse under cold running water. Peel and thinly slice peaches.

3 Just before serving, combine baby greens, watercress, orange pepper, red onion, and sliced peaches in a large bowl. Add dressing and toss gently until coated.

4 Arrange the salad on 4 plates and top each with sliced grilled chicken. Garnish with cashews and cilantro.

Grilled Chicken & Strawberry Salad with Creamy Tarragon Dressing

• 4 MAIN-COURSE SERVINGS •

Here is my version of a delicious salad we enjoyed on a recent trip to Ajijic, Mexico. Green pumpkin seeds, also known as pepitas, *add crunch and great flavour. Brushing the chicken with a little dressing while grilling will keep it moist and succulent.*

INGREDIENTS

- 1 cup (250 mL) low-fat yogurt
- ¼ cup (60 mL) low-fat mayonnaise
- ¼ cup (60 mL) fresh orange juice
- 2 Tbsp (30 mL) chopped fresh tarragon
- 2 Tbsp (30 mL) minced shallots
- 2 Tbsp (30 mL) apple cider vinegar
- 1 tsp (5 mL) honey Dijon mustard
- sea salt and freshly ground pepper

- 4 skinless, boneless chicken breasts

- 2 cups (500 mL) baby spinach
- 1 head Boston lettuce, torn, or mixed baby greens
- 2 cups (500 mL) strawberries, hulled and sliced
- ½ cup (125 mL) toasted pumpkin seeds or pine nuts (see tip page 8)

1. **FOR THE DRESSING:** whisk together yogurt, mayonnaise, orange juice, tarragon, shallots, vinegar, and mustard in a small bowl. Season with salt and pepper to taste. Remove ¼ cup (60 mL) dressing to a separate bowl for brushing over chicken. Set remaining dressing aside.

2. Coat barbecue grill, indoor grill, or grill pan with cooking spray. Preheat barbecue or grill to medium-high. Grill chicken, brushing frequently with dressing, about 3 to 4 minutes per side, or until cooked through. Set aside to cool, then slice.

3. Just before serving, combine spinach, lettuce, and strawberries in a large bowl and toss with just enough dressing to coat. Divide among 4 plates. Top with chicken slices and sprinkle with pumpkin seeds. Serve with remaining dressing on the side.

Tex-Mex Grilled Chicken Salad with Salsa Dressing

This is a wonderful summer salad that everyone will love. I often make it at the cottage for casual entertaining. Cajun spice, a blend of chili powder, ground cumin, cayenne, garlic, and onion, is great on chicken. I also like to add grilled corn on the cob when it's in season, cut into 2-inch (5 cm) pieces. Serve this salad with a basket of baked tortilla chips on the side.

INGREDIENTS

1 Tbsp (15 mL) Cajun spice	½ cup (125 mL) low-fat sour cream or yogurt
¼ cup (60 mL) fresh lime or lemon juice	½ cup (125 mL) salsa
½ cup (125 mL) grapeseed or safflower oil	2 Tbsp (30 mL) fresh lime juice
2 zucchini, cut in half	sea salt and freshly ground pepper
1 sweet red pepper, cut in quarters	
1 sweet yellow pepper, cut in quarters	1 ripe but firm avocado, pitted, peeled, and sliced (see tip page 5; prepare just before serving)
1 large red onion, sliced in ½-inch (1 cm) rounds	
6 small boneless, skinless chicken breasts	¼ cup (60 mL) chopped fresh cilantro

1. Combine Cajun spice, lime juice, and oil in a small bowl. Brush half the mixture onto the zucchini, red and yellow peppers, and onion slices and the remaining half onto the chicken breasts. Set aside to marinate for 30 minutes.

2. **FOR THE DRESSING**: combine sour cream, salsa, and lime juice in a small bowl. Season with salt and pepper to taste and set aside. If making ahead, cover and refrigerate for up to 2 days.

3. Preheat barbecue grill to medium-high heat. Place vegetables on the grill. Grill for 3 to 4 minutes per side, or until vegetables are tender-crisp. Remove to a cutting board. When cool enough to handle, slice vegetables and arrange them on a large platter.

4. Grill chicken for 3 to 4 minutes per side, until no longer pink inside. When cool enough to handle, slice chicken and place on top of vegetables.

5. Just before serving, divide avocado slices and place them on either side of the platter. Scatter cilantro over the salad. Serve with salsa dressing on the side.

Never be bored, and you will never be boring. —ELEANOR ROOSEVELT

Crispy Chicken with Arugula & Parmesan

Crispy, tender, warm chicken on a bed of arugula is absolutely delightful!
This is a favourite dish inspired by a salad I enjoyed in Italy.

INGREDIENTS

4 boneless, skinless chicken breast halves

¼ tsp (1 mL) sea salt

¼ tsp (1 mL) freshly ground pepper

½ cup (125 mL) all-purpose flour

1 large egg

1½ cups (375 mL) dry breadcrumbs,
    preferably panko (Japanese
    breadcrumbs)

2 Tbsp (30 mL) butter, divided

2 Tbsp (30 mL) extra virgin olive oil, divided

3 Tbsp (45 mL) fresh lemon juice

¼ cup (60 mL) extra virgin olive oil

generous grind of fresh pepper

8 cups (2 L) baby arugula

½ cup (125 mL) coarsely grated fresh
    Parmesan cheese

1. Pound chicken between 2 sheets of waxed paper or plastic wrap to a thickness of ¼ inch (6 mm). Season with salt and pepper.

2. Place flour on a plate, whisk egg in a medium bowl, and place breadcrumbs on another plate. Dip each piece of chicken first in flour, then in egg, and last in breadcrumbs to evenly coat each side. Lay the breaded breasts on a sheet of waxed paper.

3. Preheat the oven to 350°F (180°C). Heat 1 Tbsp (15 mL) butter and 1 Tbsp (15 mL) olive oil in a large skillet over medium-high heat. When the oil sizzles, place 2 chicken breasts in the skillet and pan-fry until golden, about 2 minutes; gently turn over with tongs and cook until the second side is golden brown, about 2 more minutes. Drain on paper towels and set aside. Wipe skillet with a paper towel and repeat with the remaining butter, olive oil, and chicken. Place all the crispy chicken on a baking sheet and bake until cooked through, about 6 minutes.

4. **FOR THE VINAIGRETTE:** whisk together lemon juice, olive oil, and pepper to taste in a small bowl. Set aside.

5. Just before serving, place arugula in a large bowl and toss with vinaigrette. Add Parmesan and toss lightly. Arrange the salad on 4 plates and top each with crispy chicken.

TIP Look for panko breadcrumbs in the Asian section of your supermarket or at an Asian market.

Chicken BLT Salad with Creamy Herb Dressing

• 4 MAIN-COURSE SERVINGS •

This salad has all the fixings of a BLT sandwich, with added protein from chicken and eggs. Wondering what to do with extra buttermilk? One of my favourite soup recipes from For the Love of Soup *is Carrot Vichyssoise, made with buttermilk—a creamy and delicious chilled soup that would go well with this salad as a first course.*

INGREDIENTS

½ cup (125 mL) buttermilk

½ cup (125 mL) low-fat sour cream or yogurt

2 Tbsp (30 mL) low-fat mayonnaise

2 Tbsp (30 mL) fresh lemon juice

2 Tbsp (30 mL) finely chopped fresh tarragon

2 Tbsp (30 mL) finely chopped fresh parsley

2 Tbsp (30 mL) finely chopped shallots

sea salt and freshly ground pepper

3 cups (750 mL) bite-sized chunks cooked chicken (about 1 small deli-roasted chicken, skinned)

6 bacon slices, cooked until crisp and crumbled

2 tomatoes, lightly seeded and cut in wedges

1 small English cucumber, cut in half and sliced

½ cup (125 mL) thinly sliced red onion

4 cups (1 L) baby spinach

1 romaine heart, torn into bite-sized pieces

4 chilled hard-boiled eggs, quartered (see tip page 8)

½ cup (125 mL) crumbled blue cheese (optional)

1 **FOR THE DRESSING**: combine buttermilk, sour cream, mayonnaise, lemon juice, tarragon, parsley, and shallots in a small bowl. Add salt and pepper to taste and set aside. If making ahead, cover and refrigerate up to 2 days.

2 Just before serving, place chicken, bacon, tomatoes, cucumber, red onion, spinach, and romaine in a large serving bowl. Toss with just enough dressing to coat. Gently toss in eggs and cheese (if using). Serve with extra dressing on the side.

TIP You can prepare the bacon, eggs, and all other ingredients earlier in the day. Store in individual containers or Ziploc bags until ready to serve.

New York Cobb Salad

My daughter and I had our first taste of Cobb salad in New York City. It was the largest salad ever put in front of us, and also the most expensive. This is my version of the classic Cobb salad, which was originally developed at a Hollywood restaurant.

INGREDIENTS

2 tsp (10 mL) Dijon mustard

2 Tbsp (30 mL) finely chopped shallots

2 Tbsp (30 mL) sherry vinegar or red wine vinegar

2 Tbsp (30 mL) fresh lemon juice

1 tsp (5 mL) Worcestershire sauce

½ cup (125 mL) extra virgin olive oil

sea salt and freshly ground pepper

2 cups (500 mL) diced or shredded cooked chicken

2 hard-boiled eggs, chilled, and sliced or coarsely chopped (see tip page 8)

½ cup (125 mL) diced black forest ham, OR 4 slices bacon, cooked and crumbled

6 cups (1.5 L) torn heart of romaine lettuce

2 cups (500 mL) watercress, larger stems removed, or baby arugula

1 ripe but firm avocado, peeled, pitted, and diced (see tip page 5; prepare just before serving, or toss with a little lemon juice to prevent browning)

1 cup (250 mL) cherry or grape tomatoes, halved

3 green onions, finely chopped

1 cup (250 mL) crumbled blue cheese

1 **FOR THE DRESSING**: combine mustard, shallots, vinegar, lemon juice, and
   Worcestershire sauce in a small bowl. Gradually whisk in oil until well combined,
   and season with salt and pepper to taste. Set aside, or if making ahead, cover and
   refrigerate up to 4 days.

2 Just before serving, combine chicken, eggs, ham, lettuce, watercress, avocado,
   cherry tomatoes, green onions, and blue cheese in a large salad bowl. Toss gently
   with dressing.

TIP You can prepare all ingredients earlier in the day and store them separately in
airtight containers or Ziploc bags.

Five-Spice Grilled Pork Tenderloin & Noodle Salad

This Asian-inspired salad is delicious and unique, with intriguing flavours and textures in every bite. Lean pork tenderloin is easy to grill when butterflied; you can also substitute chicken or shrimp. Whole wheat pasta is a good source of fibre and has an appealing chewiness.

INGREDIENTS

¼ cup (60 mL) fresh orange juice

¼ cup (60 mL) low-sodium soy sauce

¼ cup (60 mL) unseasoned rice wine vinegar

2 Tbsp (30 mL) brown sugar

2 garlic cloves, minced

1 Tbsp (15 mL) grated fresh ginger

2 tsp (10 mL) five-spice powder (see tip)

1 tsp (5 mL) orange zest

¼ cup (60 mL) grapeseed or safflower oil

2 small pork tenderloins, trimmed of excess fat and silverskin

10 oz (300 g) dry whole wheat spaghettini

2 cups (500 mL) bean sprouts or shredded napa cabbage

1 ripe mango, diced (see tip page 5)

1 small cucumber, cut into thin matchsticks

2 carrots, coarsely grated

3 green onions, finely chopped

⅓ cup (80 mL) chopped fresh cilantro or flat-leaf parsley

¼ cup (60 mL) chopped fresh mint

1 **FOR THE DRESSING (AND PORK MARINADE):** combine orange juice, soy sauce, vinegar, brown sugar, garlic, ginger, five-spice powder, and orange zest in a small bowl. Gradually whisk in oil until well combined. Set aside.

2 Cut tenderloins in half lengthwise, almost but not all the way through; open like a book. Place in a Ziploc bag or in a shallow glass bowl with half the dressing and let marinate for 30 minutes, or for several hours in the refrigerator.

3 Meanwhile, bring a large saucepan of salted water to a boil. Add spaghettini and cook until al dente. Place in a large serving bowl, toss with remaining dressing, and set aside.

4 Brush a barbecue grill, indoor grill, or grill pan with cooking spray. Preheat barbecue or grill to medium-high. Grill tenderloins for 5 to 6 minutes per side, until no longer pink inside. Remove from grill and let sit for 5 minutes. Slice tenderloins into thin strips.

5 Toss bean sprouts, mango, cucumber, carrots, green onions, cilantro, mint, and grilled pork with noodles. Can be served at room temperature or chilled. If making ahead, cover and refrigerate for up to 2 days.

TIP Five-spice powder is a blend of ground fennel seeds, Szechuan peppercorns, cinnamon, star anise, and cloves. It is available in the spice section of well-stocked supermarkets.

Grilled Lamb Salad with Olives, Feta, Mint & Crispy Pita

This salad is so easy, yet so sophisticated. I love the combination of olives, feta, and mint with lamb. Crispy pita completes this wonderful meal.

INGREDIENTS

2 lb (1 kg) boneless, butterflied leg of lamb

extra virgin olive oil for brushing

1 garlic clove, minced

1 Tbsp (15 mL) chopped fresh rosemary, OR 1 tsp (5 mL) dried rosemary

freshly ground pepper

1 tsp (5 mL) Dijon mustard

1 large garlic clove, minced

2 Tbsp (30 mL) fresh lemon juice

1 Tbsp (15 mL) sherry vinegar or red wine vinegar

¼ cup (60 mL) extra virgin olive oil

sea salt and freshly ground pepper

2 whole wheat pita breads, split horizontally and halved

extra virgin olive oil for brushing

sea salt and freshly ground pepper

6 cups (1.5 L) torn heart of romaine lettuce

1 bunch watercress, larger stems removed (optional)

1 small English cucumber, halved lengthwise and sliced

1 cup (250 mL) grape tomatoes or cherry tomatoes, halved

2 green onions, finely chopped

⅓ cup (80 mL) kalamata olives or oil-cured black olives, pitted and sliced

½ cup (125 mL) diced feta

¼ cup (60 mL) coarsely chopped fresh mint

1　Trim fat from lamb and brush with a mixture of olive oil, garlic, and rosemary. Season with pepper. Allow to sit at room temperature for 30 minutes.

2　**FOR THE VINAIGRETTE**: combine mustard, garlic, lemon juice, and vinegar in a small bowl. Gradually whisk in olive oil until well combined, and season with salt and pepper to taste. Set aside.

3　Preheat barbecue grill to medium-high heat.

4　Place lamb on grill and brown 6 minutes per side. Meanwhile, preheat oven to 350°F (180°C). Transfer lamb to a baking pan and roast in the oven for about 30 minutes longer, turning once during the cooking time, until a meat thermometer reads 150°F (66°C) for medium-rare, or until done to your preference. Remove from oven and allow lamb to rest for several minutes before slicing.

5　Brush pitas with olive oil and sprinkle with salt and pepper to taste. Grill for 1 to 2 minutes per side, or until golden and crisp. Set aside.

6　Just before serving, combine romaine, watercress (if using), cucumber, tomatoes, green onions, olives, feta, and mint in a large bowl. Add vinaigrette and toss to coat. Divide the salad among 4 plates. Top each with slices of lamb and serve with crispy grilled pita on the side.

TIP You can also use an indoor grill or grill pan to sear the lamb before transferring to the oven to roast. The pita can also be cut into wedges and baked in the oven for about 12 minutes, or until golden and crisp.

Seafood Salads

Cajun Grilled Halibut with Corn & Black Bean Salad

My husband and I encountered this creative, delicious salad at a wonderful restaurant in Toronto. I came up with my own version and have received rave reviews from friends. Halibut is a thick, juicy fish that is wonderful when grilled; you can substitute grouper or swordfish, if you prefer.

INGREDIENTS

four 6 oz (175 g) halibut fillets
2   Tbsp (30 mL) extra virgin olive oil
2   tsp (10 mL) Cajun spice

3   cobs fresh corn
extra virgin olive oil for brushing

19 oz (540 mL) can black beans, drained
    and rinsed
1   jalapeño pepper, seeded and finely chopped
1   garlic clove, minced
¼   cup (60 mL) chopped fresh cilantro or
    flat-leaf parsley
3   Tbsp (45 mL) fresh lime juice
2   Tbsp (30 mL) extra virgin olive oil
sea salt and freshly ground pepper

1 Preheat barbecue or indoor grill to medium-high heat.

2 Brush halibut fillets with olive oil and sprinkle with Cajun spice. Set aside.

3 Shuck corn and brush lightly with olive oil. Place corn on grill and cook for 12 to 15 minutes, until golden brown on all sides, turning frequently. Remove from heat and set aside to cool.

4 Meanwhile, combine black beans, jalapeño, garlic, cilantro, lime juice, and oil in a large bowl. Season to taste with salt and pepper.

5 Place halibut fillets on grill and cook for 5 to 6 minutes on each side, or until fish is slightly opaque in the centre.

6 Scrape kernels off corn cobs with a serrated knife and add to black bean mixture.

7 Place corn and bean salad on a large platter or divide among 4 individual plates, and top with grilled fish. The corn and black bean salad can be made ahead, covered, and refrigerated up to 3 days.

Grilled Swordfish Brochette with Orange Vinaigrette

*Impress your guests with this gorgeous salad! The key
to moist and tender grilled swordfish is to undercook it slightly.*

INGREDIENTS

metal or wooden skewers (if using wooden
skewers, soak in water for 30 minutes)

½ cup (125 mL) dry white wine or vermouth
2 Tbsp (30 mL) extra virgin olive oil
2 garlic cloves, minced
1½ lb (750 g) swordfish, 1 inch (2.5 cm) thick
freshly ground pepper

1 tsp (5 mL) Dijon mustard
1 garlic clove, minced
1 tsp (5 mL) orange zest

¼ cup (60 mL) fresh orange juice
2 Tbsp (30 mL) fresh lemon juice
2 tsp (10 mL) liquid honey
1 Tbsp (15 mL) chopped fresh flat-leaf parsley
1 tsp (5 mL) fresh thyme
3 Tbsp (45 mL) extra virgin olive oil
sea salt and freshly ground pepper

6 cups (1.5 L) red leaf lettuce, Boston
lettuce, or mixed baby greens
1 sweet red pepper, thinly sliced
2 green onions, finely chopped

1   Combine white wine, olive oil, and garlic in a medium bowl. Cut swordfish into 1½-inch (4 cm) chunks and add to wine mixture. Toss well to thoroughly coat. Let marinate for 20 to 30 minutes. Thread swordfish onto skewers and season with pepper.

2   **FOR THE VINAIGRETTE**: combine mustard, garlic, orange zest, orange juice, lemon juice, honey, parsley, and thyme in a small bowl. Gradually whisk in olive oil until well combined, and season with salt and pepper to taste. Set aside. If making ahead, cover and refrigerate for up to 4 days.

3   Grease a barbecue grill, indoor grill, or grill pan and preheat to medium-high. Place skewers on grill and cook for approximately 6 minutes, turning every 2 minutes, until fish is opaque in the centre. Do not overcook.

4   Combine lettuce, red pepper, and green onions in a large bowl. Toss with just enough vinaigrette to coat. Divide the salad among 4 plates and top each with grilled swordfish skewers. Pass around remaining vinaigrette to use on both the salad and the swordfish.

Cooking is at once one of the simplest and most gratifying of the arts, but to cook well one must love and respect food. —CRAIG CLAIBORNE

Grilled Tuna Niçoise

There is nothing tastier than a niçoise salad made with freshly grilled tuna. This spring version of niçoise features fresh asparagus and chives.

INGREDIENTS

1   tsp (5 mL) Dijon mustard
2   garlic cloves, minced
2   Tbsp (30 mL) finely chopped shallots
2   Tbsp (30 mL) chopped fresh dill
    or tarragon
3   Tbsp (45 mL) fresh lemon juice
⅓   cup (80 mL) extra virgin olive oil
sea salt and freshly ground pepper

16 asparagus spears, trimmed

8   small red potatoes, halved
½   tsp (2 mL) sea salt

1   lb (500 g) fresh tuna steak

4   cups (1 L) mixed baby greens
4   hard-boiled eggs, chilled, peeled,
    and quartered (see tip page 8)
1   cup halved grape or cherry tomatoes
2   Tbsp (30 mL) coarsely chopped fresh chives
2   Tbsp (30 mL) capers, drained and rinsed, OR
    8 anchovy fillets, coarsely chopped
12 niçoise or oil-cured black olives

1. **FOR THE VINAIGRETTE**: combine mustard, garlic, shallots, dill, and lemon juice in a small bowl. Gradually whisk in olive oil until well combined, and season with salt and pepper to taste. Set aside. If making ahead, cover and refrigerate up to 4 days.

2. Cook asparagus in a large skillet of boiling, salted water for 2 to 3 minutes, or until tender but firm. Drain asparagus, rinse under cold water, and pat dry on paper towels. Set aside.

3. Place potatoes in a large saucepan. Add enough water to cover by 1 inch (2.5 cm). Sprinkle with salt. Bring to a boil and cook until potatoes are tender, 8 to 10 minutes. Drain. Let cool for 5 minutes, then add 2 Tbsp (30 mL) of the vinaigrette while the potatoes are still warm. Toss to coat. Season with salt and pepper to taste and set aside.

4. Grease a barbecue grill, indoor grill, or grill pan with cooking spray and preheat to medium-high. Grill tuna for approximately 2 minutes per side, or until done to your preference, but do not overcook. Cut into thick slices.

5. Just before serving, place mixed baby greens on individual serving plates. Arrange asparagus, potatoes, eggs, tomatoes, chives, capers, and olives decoratively on top of each salad. Place tuna slices in the centre of each salad and drizzle remaining vinaigrette overtop.

TIP If making ahead, prepare vinaigrette, potatoes (tossed with 2 Tbsp/30 mL of vinaigrette while still warm), and asparagus earlier in the day and refrigerate, covered. Bring to room temperature before serving. You can replace the fresh tuna with two 6 oz (170 g) cans of albacore tuna, drained.

Grilled Salmon & Asparagus Salad
with Creamy Horseradish Dressing

Creamy horseradish dressing is divine with salmon and asparagus! Salmon is an excellent source of protein and vitamin D, as well as omega-3 and omega-6 fatty acids.

INGREDIENTS

¼ cup (60 mL) low-fat sour cream

¼ cup (60 mL) buttermilk or low-fat milk

3 Tbsp (45 mL) fresh lemon juice

2 Tbsp (30 mL) low-fat mayonnaise

2 Tbsp (30 mL) finely chopped shallots

2 Tbsp (30 mL) finely chopped fresh flat-leaf parsley

1 Tbsp (15 mL) creamy horseradish

1 tsp (5 mL) Dijon mustard

sea salt and freshly ground pepper

four 6 oz (175 g) centre-cut salmon fillets, skin on

1 bunch asparagus, trimmed

1 Tbsp (15 mL) extra virgin olive oil

freshly ground pepper

6 cups (1.5 L) mixed baby greens

1 bunch watercress, larger stems removed

½ English cucumber, chopped

1 cup (250 mL) grape or cherry tomatoes, halved

2 green onions, thinly sliced

1 **FOR THE DRESSING:** whisk together sour cream, buttermilk, lemon juice, mayonnaise, shallots, parsley, horseradish, and mustard in a small bowl. Season with salt and pepper to taste and set aside. If making ahead, cover and refrigerate up to 2 days.

2 Grease barbecue grill and preheat to medium-high. Brush salmon and asparagus with oil. Sprinkle generously with pepper. Place salmon, skin side down, and asparagus on barbecue grill, close lid, and grill until fish flakes easily when tested and asparagus is tender-crisp, about 8 to 10 minutes. When cool enough to handle, remove skin from salmon.

3 Meanwhile, combine baby greens, watercress, cucumber, tomatoes, and green onions in a large bowl. Toss with just enough dressing to coat. Divide salad among 4 plates and top each with asparagus and grilled salmon. Serve with remaining dressing.

TIP Instead of using the barbecue, you can roast the salmon and the asparagus in the oven. Preheat oven to 450°F (230°C). Brush asparagus and salmon with olive oil and season with salt and pepper. Place asparagus and salmon, skin side down, on a baking sheet. Roast in centre of preheated oven for 10 to 12 minutes.

Hoisin-Glazed Salmon with Couscous & Asparagus Salad

Tossing a piece of salmon on the grill is one of the quickest routes to a healthy, delicious dinner. The hoisin glaze gives the fish a wonderful caramelized coating. A bed of fluffy couscous with asparagus and peppers in orange-flavoured vinaigrette completes this lovely meal.

INGREDIENTS

1¼ cups (310 mL) low-sodium chicken stock or water

1 cup (250 mL) couscous

16 asparagus spears, trimmed and cut into 2-inch (5 cm) pieces

3 Tbsp (45 mL) finely chopped shallots

3 Tbsp (45 mL) fresh lemon juice

2 Tbsp (30 mL) grapeseed or safflower oil

sea salt and freshly ground pepper

2 Tbsp (30 mL) hoisin sauce

2 Tbsp (30 mL) fresh orange juice

1 Tbsp (15 mL) grapeseed or safflower oil

1 tsp (5 mL) finely grated fresh ginger

four 6 oz (175 g) centre-cut salmon fillets, skin removed

1 yellow pepper, cut into thin strips

1 navel orange, cut in sections (optional) (see tip page 5)

2 Tbsp (30 mL) chopped fresh cilantro or flat-leaf parsley

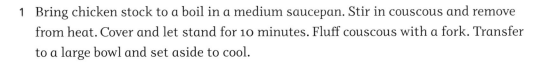

1   Bring chicken stock to a boil in a medium saucepan. Stir in couscous and remove from heat. Cover and let stand for 10 minutes. Fluff couscous with a fork. Transfer to a large bowl and set aside to cool.

2   Cook asparagus in a small amount of boiling water for 2 to 3 minutes, or until tender-crisp. Drain asparagus, rinse under cold water, and pat dry on paper towels. Set aside.

3   **FOR THE VINAIGRETTE**: combine shallots and lemon juice in a small bowl. Whisk in oil until well combined. Season with salt and pepper to taste and set aside.

4   Coat barbecue grill, indoor grill, or grill pan with cooking spray and preheat to medium-high. Combine hoisin sauce, orange juice, grapeseed oil, and ginger in a small bowl. Brush each salmon fillet with hoisin mixture. Grill salmon for 3 to 4 minutes on each side, or until fish flakes easily when tested.

5   Combine asparagus, pepper strips, orange sections (if using), and cilantro with couscous and toss with vinaigrette. Divide couscous salad among 4 individual plates or place on a large platter, and top with grilled salmon. If making ahead, couscous salad can be covered and refrigerated for up to 3 days; add salmon just before serving. Best served at room temperature.

TIP The salmon can be added to the couscous salad hot off the grill, at room temperature, or chilled.

Smoked Salmon & Asparagus Salad
with Creamy Horseradish Dressing

This is an elegant starter or luncheon salad your guests will love, especially if you serve it with a chilled bottle of Chardonnay and a basket of warm or toasted bread. For a beautiful presentation, garnish with nasturtiums or other edible flowers.

INGREDIENTS

16 to 20 asparagus stalks, trimmed
(about 1 lb/500 g)

¼ cup (60 mL) low-fat yogurt or
sour cream

2 Tbsp (30 mL) low-fat mayonnaise

1 Tbsp (15 mL) horseradish

1 Tbsp (15 mL) grainy Dijon mustard

2 Tbsp (30 mL) fresh lemon juice

1 Tbsp (15 mL) finely chopped
fresh dill

1 Tbsp (15 mL) finely chopped fresh
flat-leaf parsley

sea salt and freshly ground pepper

8 lettuce leaves (red leaf or
Boston lettuce)

12 slices smoked salmon
(about 8 oz/250 g)

2 green onions, thinly sliced

coarsely chopped fresh dill

4 lemon wedges

1 Cook whole asparagus in a skillet of boiling water just until tender-crisp. Drain asparagus, rinse under cold water, and pat dry on paper towels. Set aside.

2 **FOR THE DRESSING:** whisk together yogurt, mayonnaise, horseradish, mustard, lemon juice, dill, and parsley in a small bowl. Season with salt and pepper to taste and set aside. If making ahead, cover and refrigerate up to 2 days.

3 Just before serving, divide lettuce leaves and asparagus among 4 plates. Loosely fold salmon overtop, and sprinkle with green onions and dill. Garnish with lemon wedges. Serve with salad dressing on the side.

Smoked Salmon, Avocado & Egg Salad

• 4 SERVINGS •

Create a special starter or luncheon salad with peppery greens and creamy avocado, draped with smoked salmon and topped with dark croutons—delicious!

INGREDIENTS

1 tsp (5 mL) honey Dijon mustard

2 Tbsp (30 mL) finely chopped red or green onion

3 Tbsp (45 mL) fresh lemon juice

¼ cup (60 mL) extra virgin olive oil

sea salt and freshly ground pepper

4 cups (1 L) mixed greens (arugula, watercress, baby spinach, baby romaine)

1 large ripe but firm avocado, pitted, peeled, and sliced (see tip page 5; prepare just before serving)

12 slices smoked salmon (about 8 oz/250 g)

2 hard-boiled eggs, chilled, chopped (see tip page 8)

2 Tbsp (30 mL) capers, rinsed

2 cups (500 mL) pumpernickel or sourdough croutons (**see** tip page 9)

4 lemon wedges

fresh chives, cut into 2-inch (5 cm) lengths

1 **FOR THE VINAIGRETTE:** combine mustard, onion, and lemon juice in a small bowl. Gradually whisk in olive oil until well combined, and season with salt and pepper to taste. Set aside. If making ahead, cover and refrigerate up to 4 days.

2 Just before serving, place mixed greens in a large bowl and toss with just enough vinaigrette to coat. Divide the salad among 4 plates and top with avocado slices. Loosely fold salmon over the salad and sprinkle with chopped eggs and capers. Drizzle remaining vinaigrette overtop and garnish with croutons, lemon wedges, and chives.

Smoked Trout Salad with Endive & Apple

• 4 SERVINGS •

This is a delicious salad to serve as a starter to an elegant dinner. Add slices of avocado for a light main-course meal. Subtly flavoured, sleek, and supple, smoked trout is delicious served with fresh bread or pita crisps (see tip page 9).

INGREDIENTS

½ lb (250 g) smoked trout

1 tsp (5 mL) Dijon mustard
1 Tbsp (15 mL) minced fresh flat-leaf parsley
2 Tbsp (30 mL) fresh lemon juice
3 Tbsp (30 mL) extra virgin olive oil
1 Tbsp (15 mL) walnut oil or additional extra virgin olive oil
sea salt and freshly ground pepper

3 cups (750 mL) field greens or mixed baby greens
2 Belgian endives, cut lengthwise and sliced into strips
1 apple, cut into thin wedges (prepare just before serving)
2 Tbsp (30 mL) chopped chives or green onions

1 Remove any skin and bones from the trout and flake into bite-sized pieces. Set aside.

2 **FOR THE VINAIGRETTE:** combine mustard, parsley, and lemon juice in a small bowl. Gradually whisk in olive and walnut oils until well combined. Season with salt and pepper to taste and set aside.

3 Combine greens, endives, apple, and chives in a large bowl and toss with vinaigrette.

4 Arrange salad among 4 plates and top each with smoked trout.

Surimi Crab Salad with Creamy Caesar Dressing

Imitation crab, also called surimi, *is sweet, moist, tender, and delicious. It's made from a variety of white fish, mainly pollock. Substitute cooked shrimp or chicken if desired.*

INGREDIENTS

12 to 16 asparagus spears, trimmed and cut diagonally into 2-inch (5 cm) pieces

½ cup (125 mL) buttermilk, sour cream, or yogurt
¼ cup (60 mL) low-fat mayonnaise
2 Tbsp (30 mL) fresh lemon juice
1 garlic clove, minced
2 tsp (10 mL) drained capers
1 tsp (5 mL) Worcestershire sauce
sea salt and freshly ground pepper

2 romaine hearts, torn into bite-sized pieces

1 lb (500 g) surimi crab, flaked
2 cups (500 mL) sourdough croutons (see tip page 9)
½ cup (125 mL) coarsely grated fresh Parmesan cheese

1 Cook asparagus in a small amount of boiling water for 2 to 3 minutes, or until tender but firm. Drain asparagus, rinse under cold water, and pat dry on paper towels. Set aside.

2 **FOR THE DRESSING**: whisk together buttermilk, mayonnaise, lemon juice, garlic, capers, and Worcestershire sauce in a small bowl. Season with salt and pepper to taste and set aside. If making ahead, cover and refrigerate up to 2 days.

3 Just before serving, combine romaine and asparagus in a large bowl and toss with just enough dressing to coat.

4 Divide salad among 4 plates. Top each with surimi, croutons, and Parmesan cheese. Serve with remaining dressing.

A man travels the world over in search of what he needs and returns home to find it. —GEORGE MOORE

Lobster & Shrimp Salad with Creamy Tarragon Dressing

This is a sophisticated, colourful, and luscious salad. My husband requests it on special occasions. Serve with warm toasted bread or pita crisps (see tip page 9).

INGREDIENTS

¼ cup (60 mL) low-fat sour cream or buttermilk

¼ cup (60 mL) low-fat mayonnaise

2 Tbsp (30 mL) fresh orange juice

2 Tbsp (30 mL) fresh lemon juice

2 tsp (10 mL) chopped fresh tarragon

½ tsp (2 mL) Dijon mustard

sea salt and freshly ground pepper

2 cooked lobster tails, chilled

2 Belgian endives, cut lengthwise and sliced into strips

8 medium shrimp, cooked, peeled, and chilled

1 tomato, halved, seeded, and cut into strips

1 ripe but firm avocado, pitted, peeled, and sliced (see tip page 5)

2 Tbsp (30 mL) chopped fresh chives or green onions

1 Tbsp (15 mL) capers, rinsed

1 **FOR THE DRESSING**: whisk together sour cream, mayonnaise, orange juice, lemon juice, tarragon, and mustard in a small bowl. Season with salt and pepper to taste and set aside.

2 Remove meat from each lobster shell in 1 piece. Slice crosswise into thin slices. Set aside.

3 Toss endives with half the dressing and pile in serving plates. Scatter lobster, shrimp, tomato strips, avocado slices, chives, and capers on top of endives and drizzle with remaining dressing.

Shrimp Salad with Avocado, Mango & Watercress

• 4 TO 6 SERVINGS •

Marinating succulent shrimp in a ginger-orange dressing gives them a wonderful flavour. This is a striking salad that is elegant and incredibly easy to make. It is perfect for a dinner party. Serve with a basket of bread and a bottle of your favourite white wine.

INGREDIENTS

1 Tbsp (15 mL) Dijon mustard

1 tsp (5 mL) grated fresh ginger

1 tsp (5 mL) orange zest

2 Tbsp (30 mL) fresh orange juice

2 Tbsp (30 mL) champagne vinegar or good-quality white wine vinegar

1 Tbsp (15 mL) liquid honey

3 Tbsp (45 mL) extra virgin olive oil

freshly ground pepper

24 small to medium shrimp, uncooked, peeled and deveined

1 bunch watercress, larger stems removed

1 large mango, peeled and diced (see tip page 5)

2 ripe but firm avocados, pitted, peeled, and diced (see tip page 5)

1 sweet red pepper, diced

¼ cup (60 mL) finely chopped red onion

2 Tbsp (30 mL) chopped fresh mint

1 **FOR THE DRESSING:** combine mustard, ginger, orange zest, orange juice, vinegar, and honey in a small bowl. Whisk in olive oil until well combined, and season with pepper to taste. Set aside. If making ahead, cover and refrigerate up to 4 days.

2 Add 3 Tbsp (45 mL) dressing to the shrimp and let marinate in the refrigerator for 20 to 30 minutes.

3 Just before serving, sauté shrimp in a hot skillet for 2 to 3 minutes, until done (tiger prawns will turn pink). Remove from heat.

4 Combine watercress, mango, avocados, red pepper, onion, and mint in a medium-sized bowl and toss with remaining dressing. Divide salad among individual plates and top each with shrimp.

153

Grilled Shrimp Caesar Salad

This wonderful salad is an ideal first course for a dinner party or for a special luncheon. It is fresh and lemony, and the hint of ginger in the dressing will have everyone guessing. Serve with thinly sliced, toasted, buttered French bread.

INGREDIENTS

six 12-inch (30 cm) metal or wooden
    skewers (if using wooden skewers,
    soak in water for at least 30 minutes)

2 tsp (10 mL) Dijon mustard
1 large garlic clove, minced
1 tsp (5 mL) minced fresh ginger
1 tsp (5 mL) lemon zest
3 Tbsp (45 mL) fresh lemon juice
1 Tbsp (15 mL) balsamic or sherry vinegar
1 tsp (5 mL) Worcestershire sauce
⅓ cup (80 mL) extra virgin olive oil
sea salt and freshly ground pepper

24 medium or large shrimp, peeled and
    deveined (1 to 1½ lb/500 to 750 g)
1 Tbsp (15 mL) extra virgin olive oil
2 Tbsp (30 mL) fresh lemon juice
1 garlic clove, minced
1 tsp (5 mL) minced fresh ginger
½ tsp (2 mL) freshly cracked pepper

2 to 3 hearts of romaine lettuce, torn
    into bite-sized pieces
½ cup (125 mL) grated fresh Parmesan
    cheese, or more to taste
6 lemon wedges

1 **FOR THE DRESSING**: combine mustard, garlic, ginger, lemon zest, lemon juice, vinegar, and Worcestershire sauce in a small bowl. Gradually whisk in olive oil until well combined, and season with salt and pepper to taste. Set aside. If making ahead, cover and refrigerate up to 4 days.

2 Preheat a grill or broiler to medium-high heat. Dry the shrimp on paper towels. Place shrimp in a bowl and toss with olive oil, lemon juice, garlic, ginger, and cracked pepper. Let sit for 10 minutes. Thread shrimp onto 6 skewers and grill or broil 2 minutes per side, or until just cooked through.

3 Just before serving, place lettuce in a large bowl and add dressing and Parmesan cheese. Toss to coat evenly. Divide salad among 6 plates. Serve each salad with a shrimp skewer and garnish with lemon wedges.

Grilled Shrimp Tabbouleh Salad

I get rave reviews with this special salad! Enjoy the tender, nutty texture of nutritious bulgur—kernels of whole wheat that have been steamed, dried, and crushed. Plump, juicy, lemon-scented shrimp make a perfect complement. This salad is wonderful for entertaining; you can prepare the tabbouleh salad ahead of time, and then all that is left to do is grill the shrimp.

INGREDIENTS

eight 8-inch (20 cm) metal or wooden
    skewers (if using wooden skewers, soak
    in water for at least 30 minutes)

2 cups (500 mL) water
1 cup (250 mL) fine bulgur wheat
    (cracked wheat)

¼ cup (60 mL) fresh lemon juice
2 Tbsp (30 mL) extra virgin olive oil
1 garlic clove, minced
sea salt and freshly ground pepper

24 medium or large shrimp, peeled
    and deveined (about 1 to 1½ lb/
    500 to 750 g)
1 Tbsp (15 mL) extra virgin olive oil
3 Tbsp (45 mL) fresh lemon juice
½ tsp (2 mL) freshly ground pepper

3 green onions, finely chopped
2 Tbsp (30 mL) finely chopped
    fresh flat-leaf parsley
2 Tbsp (30 mL) finely chopped fresh mint
⅓ cup (80 mL) finely chopped sun-dried
    tomatoes, packed in oil
1 cup (250 mL) diced feta
fresh mint
1 English cucumber, cut in half and sliced

1   Bring water to a boil in a medium saucepan. Stir in bulgur wheat and remove
    from heat. Cover and let stand until bulgur is tender and has absorbed the water,
    about 20 minutes.

2   **FOR THE VINAIGRETTE:** whisk together lemon juice, olive oil, and garlic in a small
    bowl until well combined, and season with salt and pepper to taste. Set aside.

3   Preheat a grill or broiler to medium-high. Dry the shrimp on paper towels and
    place in a bowl. Toss shrimp with oil, lemon juice, and pepper. Thread shrimp onto
    6 skewers. Grill or broil 2 minutes per side or until just cooked through.

4   Add green onions, parsley, mint, sun-dried tomatoes, and vinaigrette to the bulgur.
    Transfer to a platter and top with feta and shrimp skewers. Garnish with mint
    leaves and place cucumber slices around the edges of the platter. Serve at room
    temperature or chilled.

TIP Did you know that if you selected 80 percent of your groceries from the outer rim
of the store, they would provide you with 80 percent of your required nutrients?

Thai Shrimp & Noodle Salad

This Thai-inspired salad is bursting with flavour and makes a satisfying yet light dish. You can replace the shrimp with chicken, beef, pork, or tofu.

INGREDIENTS

8 oz (250 g) Thai rice stick noodles, ¼ inch (6 mm) thick

1 lb (500 g) medium shrimp, cooked, peeled, and deveined
1 cup (250 mL) frozen shelled edamame (see tip page 94) or green peas, cooked
1 sweet red or yellow pepper, diced
1 small jalapeño pepper, seeded and finely chopped
2 medium carrots, shredded

3 green onions, finely chopped
½ cup (125 mL) chopped fresh cilantro
¼ cup (60 mL) chopped fresh mint

¼ cup (60 mL) fresh lime juice
1 Tbsp (15 mL) low-sodium soy sauce
1 Tbsp (15 mL) brown sugar
1 garlic clove, minced
2 tsp (10 mL) minced fresh ginger
2 Tbsp (30 mL) grapeseed or safflower oil
1 Tbsp (15 mL) toasted sesame oil

1 Place noodles in a large bowl. Completely cover noodles with boiling water. Soak for 10 minutes, or until tender but still firm. Drain and rinse under cold water.

2 Meanwhile, combine shrimp, edamame, red pepper, jalapeño, carrots, onions, cilantro, and mint in a large serving bowl.

3 **FOR THE DRESSING:** combine lime juice, soy sauce, brown sugar, garlic, and ginger in a small bowl. Gradually whisk in grapeseed and sesame oils until well combined.

4 Add dressing and noodles to shrimp and vegetables. Toss gently to coat.

Index

Thank you!

The recipes in this cookbook are the result of happy times spent in the kitchen with my family: my husband, Tim; my daughter, Julie, and her husband, Fraser; my son, Dan, and his wife, Dana; and my grandchildren, Sienna and Grayson. Thanks to all of you, my salad creations have been put to the test and passed successfully! You have all showed much enthusiasm, unconditional love, and support.

Thank you: to my good friend Dorothy for her writing suggestions; to my art classmates for sharing their creativity; and to all my friends who have supported me and bought countless copies of my previous book, *For the Love of Soup*, for their friends.

My thanks must also be extended to Robert McCullough and his team at Whitecap Books, who took on the project of publishing my first cookbook and endorsed my inspiration for this book, its follow-up.